Star
Teachers
of Children
in Poverty

Kappa Delta Pi Biennial
1994–96

Star Teachers of Children in Poverty reflects the
Society's two-year study of issues and practices related to
the biennial theme of "Educators Make the Difference."
This volume is among the books that the Society
commissions each biennium to explore critical issues in
education in ways that develop new knowledge and new
understandings.

Kappa Delta Pi, an International Honor Society in
Education founded in 1911, is dedicated to scholarship and
excellence in education. The Society promotes among its
intergenerational membership of educators the
development and dissemination of worthy educational
ideas and practices, enhances the continuous growth and
leadership of its diverse membership, fosters inquiry and
reflection of significant educational issues, and maintains a
high degree of professional fellowship.

Star Teachers
of Children in Poverty

Martin Haberman
Distinguished Professor of Education
University of Wisconsin—Milwaukee

Kappa Delta Pi, an International Honor Society in Education
West Lafayette, Indiana
1995

Direct all inquiries to the Director of Publications,
Kappa Delta Pi, 3707 Woodview Trace, Indianapolis, Indiana 46268-1158.

Project Editor: Carol Bloom

Editors: Marji E. Gold-Vukson
Grant E. Mabie
Leslie S. Rebhorn

Editorial Assistant: Linda A. Heaton

Text and Cover Design: Angela Bruntlett

Library of Congress Cataloging-in-Publication Data
Haberman, Martin.
Star teachers of children in poverty/Martin Haberman. p. cm.
Includes bibliographical references and index.

ISBN 0-912099-08-9 (pbk.) $15.00
1. Teachers—United States. 2. Teachers—United States—Interviews.
3. Poor children—Education—United States. I. Kappa Delta Pi (Honor Society) II. Title.
LB1775.2.H32 1995
371.1'00973—dc20
95-21427
CIP

Printed in the United States of America

08   20   19   18   17

The author previously published pp. 86–92 as: Haberman, M. 1994. Gentle teaching in a violent society.
Reprinted with permission of *educational HORIZONS* quarterly journal, published by Pi Lambda Theta, an
international honor and professional association in education, Bloomington, IN 47407-6626.

Photography courtesy of the University of Wisconsin—Milwaukee Photographic Services:
17, **38**, 54, **69**, 79, 87, Alan Magayne-Roshak; **29**, **59**, Bill Herrick.

Call Kappa Delta Pi International Headquarters (800-284-3167) to order.
Quantity discounts for more than 20 copies.   KDP Order Code 505

Author

Martin Haberman began his career as a teacher of preschool and elementary children. After receiving his doctorate in teacher education from Columbia University, he developed the model that became the National Teacher Corps.

During the past 35 years, Dr. Haberman served as Editor of the *Journal of Teacher Education* and consultant to many public schools, universities, foundations, and associations. He has developed more teacher education programs that have prepared more teachers for children in poverty than anyone in the history of U.S. teacher education.

Dr. Haberman's extensive research, writing, and demonstration efforts have influenced certification laws in several states and the teacher selection procedures for 30 major urban school districts. He has received more than 15 special awards, including the Standard Oil Award for Excellence in College Teaching, the Corporation for Public Broadcasting Award for special service toward the advancement of public broadcasting, and the Pomeroy Award for Outstanding Contributions to Teacher Education.

The Haberman Educational Foundation in Houston, Texas, trains schools and universities to select teachers who will be effective with children in poverty, and can be reached at 1–800–667–6185.

The author of more than 200 major papers, 150 refereed articles, 20 research projects, 8 books, and 50 chapters and monographs, Dr. Haberman is Distinguished Professor of Education at the University of Wisconsin— Milwaukee. He is a member of the prestigious Laureate Chapter of Kappa Delta Pi.

Dedication

Dedicated to the star teachers of children and youth in poverty;
anonymous and unsung
by even those whose lives they save.

Acknowledgments

The author thanks the following education professionals for reading and critically analyzing earlier drafts of the manuscript.

Dawn P. Blaus
University of Southwestern Louisiana

Delores Burdick
Northeastern University

Jacquelyn Fields
Northwestern University

Lori A. Fulton
University of New Mexico

Denise Germond
Memorial School, Medford, New Jersey

Asa Hilliard, III
Georgia State University

Theresa L. Schultz
Elizabethtown College

Contents

Chapter 4   **93**

Only Decent People Can
Be Prepared to Teach

Foreword

Kappa Delta Pi sponsors projects that recognize and reward excellence in education. During the past two years, the Society has undertaken publication projects focusing on cultural diversity, new teacher induction, gifted and talented education, and substitute teaching. Martin Haberman's book, *Star Teachers of Children in Poverty,* is the most current example of a publication that focuses on important issues facing today's educators.

For the 1994–96 biennium, Kappa Delta Pi selected "Educators Make The Difference" as its theme to focus attention on the daily and long-term effects of educators. Henry Adams's statement, "Teachers affect eternity and they never know where or when this influence stops," is an appropriate way to describe the impact phenomenon of the educator. While we hear periodically of truly great educators like Socrates, Jane Addams, John Dewey, Maria Montessori, Christa McAuliffe, and Jaime Escalante, whose influence is recorded in written and motion picture form, it is important to continue the search for the functions and ideology of teachers who make the difference in school settings that present great challenges for learning—urban classrooms.

The difficulties facing students and teachers in the largest urban school districts in the United States are different from those in smaller districts. In urban schools, students are generally poor, educationally challenged, limited in language, or handicapped in other ways. Home conditions for many students may not include a parent, and the community's support for learning is neutral at best. Increasing occurrences of school violence, drug abuse, displaying weapons in school, and misbehaving reflect the social problems occurring outside the schoolhouse. When such conditions are part of a student's life, teaching and learning are significantly affected. Thus, it is important to identify the success stories of teachers and students in demanding urban classroom settings.

Large city schools are in need of teachers who are committed to making a difference in such situations. It is the star teacher who can help to counteract the special circumstances of growing up in U.S. urban areas. We must not only attract our best and brightest teachers, but also retain them in urban schools. Students in these schools need effective teachers who make a difference. Dr. Martin Haberman, Distinguished Professor of Education at the University of Wisconsin–Milwaukee, and a member of the prestigious Laureate Chapter of Kappa Delta Pi, has undertaken the important task of identifying the functions and ideology of star teachers of children in poverty.

The harsh realities of schooling in this county's largest school districts often overshadow the daily miracles performed by these star educators. While there are many examples of teachers making a positive difference in the lives of students in the largest U.S. school districts, it isn't enough. Star teachers are needed in *every* classroom, and this goal can be achieved. Thus, Dr. Haberman performs a great service to the profession by identifying the success stories of star teachers of children in poverty.

Whether you are beginning your career or completing 25 years of service in teaching, there is much to be gained by reading this book. You will be captivated by the responses of star teachers to the Haberman interviews, challenged by his views on the state of U.S. education, and feel the pride these teachers exude as they relate their classroom success stories. It is impossible to be a spectator as you read this book; you must be a player.

Wallace D. Draper
President, Kappa Delta Pi
Professor of Education
Ball State University
Muncie, Indiana

There is nothing pedestrian about Martin Haberman. There is nothing ordinary about what he does or how he thinks. Martin Haberman is one of those rare intellects and people who understand the importance of the work they do so clearly that they constantly probe at the edges of its paradigms to be certain that there is not more or better work possible.

Shifting and changing paradigms is risky business. It takes the wisdom to understand and create the new; the courage to take the scorn of those without vision; and the strength to carry along those who have vision but no courage. Most of all, it takes the kind of caring that makes any risk a reasonable one.

Martin has that kind of wisdom, that kind of courage, that kind of strength, and that kind of caring. For Martin, ultimately nothing matters except children in classrooms, especially those who haven't been learning as much as they could—and if he can help them learn more, he will face down the paradigm, credentialing body, university, or any other windmill that he must battle.

The establishment does not mean much to Martin. Children do. Martin believes children are the only investment that counts, and he has spent his remarkable career helping them learn.

People like Martin show us how to change the world. Catch his passion as you read this book. He is asking you to take a risk. He is asking you to make things better.

Peggy Gordon Elliott
President
Akron University
Akron, Ohio

Life's greatest gift

is the opportunity to throw

oneself into a job

that puts meaning and hope

into the lives

of other people.

Seizing this opportunity

is the surest way

to put meaning and hope

into one's own life.

—Martin
Haberman

Introduction

Dear Readers:

What you are about to read should help you answer the question, "Would I be able to do this?" "This" refers to teaching children in poverty from diverse cultural backgrounds in one of the 120 largest school districts in the United States, collectively serving approximately 12 million children and youth.

Five to eight percent of the teachers at each of these school districts are "star teachers"—teachers who, by all common criteria, are outstandingly successful: their students score higher on standardized tests; parents and children think they are great; principals rate them highly; other teachers regard them as outstanding; central office supervisors consider them successful; cooperating universities regard them as superior; and they evaluate themselves as outstanding teachers (Haberman 1993). By interviewing and observing urban teachers all over the United States since 1959, I have become familiar with the substantial knowledge base these stars share. By contrasting the functions performed by star teachers with the behaviors of teachers who quit or fail in the same school systems, two kinds of teacher functions have been identified: things that both stars and failures do; and things that distinguish the practices of stars from those of quitters and failures. This volume is devoted to explicating the distinctive functions performed by stars, and the ideology that undergirds their behavior. To a lesser degree there is some description of distinctive things stars *never* do that quitters or failures *sometimes* do.

I hope that readers will consider the positive functions performed by star teachers in terms of their own proclivities and dispositions. Only an individual reader will have sufficient self-knowledge to face himself or herself honestly and determine his or her likelihood of success in this form of teaching.

For the children and youth in poverty from diverse cultural backgrounds who attend urban schools, having effective teachers is a matter of life and death. These children have no life options for achieving decent lives other than by experiencing success in school. For them, the stakes involved in schooling are extremely high. Teaching in these situations is not a job, or even a career. Dealing as it does with psychological as well as physical life and death, teaching in these situations is an extraordinary life experience—a volatile, highly charged, emotionally draining, physically exhausting experience for even the most competent, experienced teacher. For beginners, to whom this volume is primarily addressed, the pressures, intensity, and emotional commitments are beyond belief and almost beyond description. The least accurate language would describe the first year of teaching in an urban school system as a manageable or even reasonable "job." Because it generates extremely high levels of emotional intensity, it is more akin to being an air traffic controller than being a "schoolteacher." A set of indescribable experiences? Yes. A "job"? No. Before you even consider the functions of star teachers and ask, "Can I do this?" you must first ask yourself whether you can function "on the edge" with children and youth consumed by the tension that comes (and never fully abates) from having unmet basic human needs for physical safety, adequate nutrition, decent health care, freedom from pain, and the nurturance of secure adults who provide care and love.

Completing a traditional program of teacher education as preparation for working in this emotional cauldron is like preparing to swim the English Channel by doing laps in the university pool. Swimming is not swimming. Having a warm shower, a clean towel, a private locker, your own lane, and a heated, guarded, chlorinated pool has nothing whatever to do with the grueling realities of eight-foot swells of freezing water for 22 miles without being certain of your direction, and persisting alone knowing that most "reasonable" people would never submit themselves to such a challenge. After all, "Why risk your health and life for no reason?" This question makes sense to quitters and failures. Stars know the reason.

"Teaching is not teaching" and "kids are not kids." Completing your first year as a fully responsible teacher in an urban school has nothing to do with having been "successful" in a college preparation program. Even if you student-taught in an urban school, you were never accountable to the parents and principal for students' learning and behavior. You were, in a very real sense, observing from a protected, safe motor launch while somebody else tried to swim the channel. You have yet to feel the emotional drain of interacting with the children, parents, teachers, principal, and staff as the responsible, accountable teacher.

This volume describes a form of teaching in which intense feelings are ever present, undergirding the teacher's every action. The warning that it takes great commitment, greater courage, and even more persistence understates the case.

Having said all that, it is important to emphasize that literally thousands of star teachers do "it" every day. Their students learn a great deal, act with respect toward themselves and others, and are in the process of becoming happy, successful, contributing citizens. These star teachers learned on the job—some with mentors, others entirely on their own. There is every reason to believe that even greater numbers of potential teachers—some now in other walks of life as well as in universities—can be selected and coached to do as well as these star teachers.

Martin Haberman
University of Wisconsin—Milwaukee
April 1995

What Star Teachers Don't Do

Before we discuss the functions or clusters of behavior that star teachers perform, it would be useful to consider some of what they don't do. Teachers who quit or fail frequently cause many of their own problems; in other cases they exacerbate situations needlessly. The following list of issues is not exhaustive. It does, however, cover the major behaviors stars report not doing or issues they downplay. I have summarized their views regarding these "hot" topics because their views seem to me to be contrary to what many teachers do, or seem to believe.

Discipline

Star teachers are not very concerned with discipline. They have a few rules, usually less than four and usually established at the beginning of each year. They are not fixated with this issue as their highest priority or even as a major concern. Indeed, on a list of 10 things they care most about, discipline might not appear at all (Fuller 1969). This is not to say that they don't face and deal with horrendous issues—everything from a youngster being murdered or facing death threats, to an acting-out youngster vying with them for control of the classroom. The fact that they live with these problems daily—even minute by minute—still does not make discipline their major concern.

There are several reasons for their view of discipline. First, they believe problems are part of their job. They begin each semester knowing they will teach some youngsters who are affected by handicapping conditions. They anticipate that horrendous home, poverty, and environmental conditions will impinge on their students. They know that inadequate health care and nutrition, and various forms of substance and physical abuse, typify the daily existence of many of their students. In short, stars assume that the reason youngsters need teachers is because there will be all manner of serious interferences with their teaching and with students' learning. Were this not the case, almost anyone could be hired to give directions, make assignments, and correct papers. Star teachers are, in this sense, very much like dentists who are not floored when a patient's open mouth reveals diseased gums or decayed teeth. They certainly don't expect to spend all day with models for tooth-paste ads. They assume problems are the reason for needing skilled practitioners. Strange as this may seem, most of the youngsters trained in traditional programs of teacher education are prepared for classes made up of "normal" children. This training leads them to create endless mental lists of problem children who shouldn't be there, or, if they are there, who need special help from other professionals or aides: the mildly retarded, the profoundly retarded, the learning disabled, the emotionally disturbed, the physically handicapped, the speech impaired, the language limited, and the "at risk."

This traditional approach to training is counterproductive for future teachers in poverty schools since it leads them to perceive a substantial number—even a majority—of "abnormal" children in every classroom. Children and youth in poverty face teachers who begin with the assumption that most of them should not be there. The truth is that the failure and quitter teachers are correct in their perception of their preservice training—they were not prepared to deal with all children in poverty schools. Indeed, they were selected and prepared to teach only those youngsters who can learn without teachers, and to regard everyone else as a "problem" someone else should have to deal with.

The second reason stars view discipline as being of little importance is that they spend relatively little time on it. Stars might be viewed as proactive disciplinarians. Their normal teaching style involves much individual interaction with students. This gives them an opportunity to learn a great deal about their students before emergencies occur (Haberman 1965). These in-depth, natural interactions around classroom activities permit stars to anticipate, prevent, or ward off many emergencies. The information they know and constantly gain from children before-hand makes it easier to deal with disciplinary or emergency situations. Knowledge about their students helps stars to teach them more, but it also cuts down on discipline problems when they do surface. It is much less likely that youngsters will lash out at teachers who know them well and who have established relationships with them. It is infinitely easier for students to make themselves problems to strangers. The point is that stars have established working relationships with children around learning activities and do not try to develop personal relationships built around discipline problems after such problems arise. Stars spend so little time on discipline because they have invested their time and effort creating learning activities that have helped them build caring relationships with each of the children.

A third reason stars do not perceive discipline as a major issue is that they expect a range of achievement in their classrooms in the same way they expect a range of behaviors. They do not begin with the failure teacher's assumption that teachers should have classes comprised of homogeneous ability groups reading on or near grade level (Haberman and Raths 1968). This means that successful teachers don't create discipline situations by assigning meaningless work. Neither do they engender hostility or resistance by assigning tasks that students have no way of doing. Indeed, stars work very hard at assigning less and less as the year progresses. In the course of their year with students, they develop more and more ways of involving the pupils in the determination of their own assignments.

Thus far several reasons have been offered for why star teachers do not regard discipline as their major problem or even as a high priority. They expect problems as part of their normal workload. They use very few rules, established early. They build strong personal relationships with children around learning tasks and do not leave the process of relating to a child until after a serious problem arises. They expect wide differences in student achievement and anticipate that many students will test below grade level. Their assignments and expectations of students do not exacerbate the condition that the typical urban classroom has a wide range of achievement levels. They act with confidence on tentatively held beliefs rather than present a frazzled, harried, or authoritarian image to their classes. Teachers who feel harried act harried. In turn, they inevitably engender stressful reactions from their pupils.

These are not rules for becoming a great disciplinarian but, rather, an analysis of how stars' perceptions of their job makes what they do different from most other teachers. There is no suggestion here that stars do not face the horrendous problems of all teachers who work with poverty children. The major difference between stars and other teachers is that most others—particularly failures and quitters—perceive discipline to be an issue separate from teaching. Most teachers see discipline as a set of procedures that must be put in place before learning can occur, and believe that few of their problems with discipline emanate from the way they teach. If they get to know children in any depth at all, it is after undesirable events have occurred. Stars perceive the reverse. They seek to establish in-depth caring relationships in the course of their day-to-day teaching activities, and to avoid, deflect, or defuse problems that would inevitably arise if such rapport had not been developed. They know this will not forestall all problems, but it will make their work manageable. The fact that they expect and plan for such problems gives them a perspective different from other teachers. Again, the difference is between treating discipline as a prior condition and a set of controls apart from how learning activities are pursued vs. using the learning activities themselves as the basis of self-control. When students are involved in an activity, they discipline themselves.

Most teachers, if asked how they would solve a discipline problem, describe the next level of escalation in some control scheme: talk to the offender, talk to the parent, talk to the principal, talk to the psychologist! Stars, on the other hand, describe the next level in terms of work: find something the student is interested in, find something else the student can do, find something else the student can share. Stars view discipline primarily as a natural consequence of their ability to interest and involve learners. Again, this is not to say they never face discipline problems separate from or prior to the work going on, but that they minimize such events.

Most teachers are sufficiently sophisticated to realize that a list of "10 easy steps" or a summary of "how to discipline" will not be very helpful to them. What they are less likely to see is that discipline does not occur entirely prior to or apart from learning. It is an integral part of how the learning and teacher-student interactions proceed. A final caveat is in order. Failure teachers and quitters frequently state: "With more than 30 in a room, retaining all this individual knowledge about each kid is impossible." This view neglects the facts. These same teachers spend endless hours during and after school with parents, principals, the offending child, guidance counselors, and others after an incident has occurred. The investment in teacher time would be much less beforehand. Poor teachers spend more time on after-the-fact discipline than stars spend on finding interesting things for children to do and interesting ways for them to learn. This fact leads me to believe that finding time for individuals is more a question of how the teacher perceives his or her work than a matter of actual time (Doyle 1985).

Punishment

Star teachers do not engage in corporal punishment, even where legal and sanctioned. They do not perceive themselves as instruments of punishment at all. This should go without saying, but it doesn't because most states still allow corporal punishment; i.e., they permit individual school districts to practice or prohibit physical punishment. The state of Texas, for example, requires that a written form be completed and filed to document each instance of physical punishment. In a typical year, over 275,000 cases are reported. Imagine how many go unreported! This issue is peculiar to the United States. There are already 12 nations in which it is illegal for parents to spank or hit their own children, while we in this country still regard the use of physical punishment as a debatable issue for instructional purposes

(Harper and Epstein 1989). Can one practice a "profession" by beating the client?

Star teachers use few punishments and generally do not think in terms of punishments. Essentially, they are not proponents of behavior modification. They do not conceive of their relationship with students in terms of rewards or punishments because they do not regard their students as animals to be shaped. Neither do they see themselves as controlling a laboratory in which all the rewards and punishments emanate from one authority (Haberman 1994). Because they know they cannot control their students' reactions or perceptions—let alone their drives—star teachers do not think of themselves as reinforcers, rewarders, shapers, or extinguishers. They think in the words of ordinary language, rather than in the jargon of the psychology lab assistant, training rats to ring bells and run mazes in order to receive water and food. Star teachers think in ways that explain, rather than mystify. *Interest, involvement,* and *participation* are more common words for them than *motivation.* Being happy for—and *with*—a youngster who does well is a more common response for them than issuing a reward. Sharing a student's feeling of accomplishment is a more common perception than reinforcing any behavior. Star teachers see themselves as working with students, coaching, and providing help. And, most of all, they think they are encouraging students to want to do the work because of its intrinsic value, not monitoring a system of extrinsic rewards. Simply stated, stars perceive punishments as examples of extrinsic control—and their goal is to foster the development of internal controls by students. The fact that stars tend to use ordinary language rather than psycho-educational jargon indicates that they see themselves as humans interacting with other humans and not as power figures controlling the behavior of others. Star teachers not only know but *accept* the reality that, ultimately, they cannot force anyone to learn.

Another reason stars do not use punishment as a primary means of control is simpler: it doesn't work. Regardless of the type of punishment, the same youngsters get most of the punishments—and few are transformed into successful students as a result (Wilson-Brewer, Cohen, O'Donnell, and Goodman 1992). Again, teachers are trained to escalate; i.e., warn, withdraw a privilege, administer a negative consequence, remove, suspend, and finally evict. Not only are such procedures ineffective, but the number of at-risk, disruptive, and failing students is skyrocketing as more and more teachers use more and more punishments. In truth, the positive rewards adolescents receive from peers for noncompliance are more powerful than any of the school's punishments (Wilson-Brewer et al. 1992).

Meting out punishments is the last refuge of those who believe they have the

Chapter 1

power to *make* people learn, i.e., compel reluctant learners to shape up. There can be no masking this essentially authoritarian philosophy. Teachers who use escalating punishments are assuming they can force people to comply and that, by such coerced obedience, they can make students learn. Children frequently sense from the earliest ages—even before they can fully comprehend the implications of what is happening to them—that they must fight for their freedom against external control over their minds, bodies, and spirits. Most children in poverty become passive resisters after the primary grades and simply keep themselves from becoming fully involved in school. They comply outwardly but resist inwardly. As a result, the 13 years they spend in school following directions and avoiding punishments develops only a fraction of their potential. It does not create self-directed learners.

Not all children in poverty respond passively to the authoritarianism of teachers who punish. As they grow in size, many fight back directly. In so doing, they are saying, in effect, "You can't make me learn. Your punishments are nothing compared to those outside of school."

To most, school punishments seem related to nonlearning behaviors, i.e., lateness, disruptions, or not following directions. Stars know better than other teachers that these offenses are symptomatic of students not being involved with meaningful learning activities.

For several years I observed teachers in a prison high school. The incarcerated adolescents were forced to attend every day and to "learn." This was accomplished with a system of very powerful rewards and punishments: water, food, privacy, forced labor, cigarettes, and the opportunity for sex. Most of the students complied and seemed to be learning. I observed students classified as retarded who could read from a screen faster than I could. Actually, they were merely calling words correctly and only *appeared* to be "reading." I don't know that they understood what they were saying. We do know that, aside from pornography, which was used as a reward, they never read during their free time, although there was an excellent library.

This experience confirmed for me the power of behavior modification to control but not to educate. The student inmates appeared to learn some things and not others. They made none of these "learned behaviors" their own. They did not become readers, word processors, or auto mechanics although they apparently demonstrated some of these specific skills while incarcerated. Even when the teaching authorities could control them with powerful rewards and punishments— short of death or mutilation—the students successfully resisted being forced to learn. They complied outwardly, but internalized little or nothing. Upon release, none finished high school. A few passed GEDs. A majority are now in prison or dead.

When I share this example with teachers, many are envious of the power of the punishments available to prison teachers. They believe that, if they had access to such powerful rewards and punishments, they might finally be able to exert some influence over their problem students. What most teachers seem to be searching for is a surefire system of increasingly powerful rewards and punishments, which could be memorized, so the teacher would then know what to do first, second, and third to compel students to learn. Stars do not fantasize about such a system. They do not believe that punishments can, in any real sense, be educative. They use them only as a last resort, and recognize that punishments indicate a failure on their part, or that they may have given up on a youngster. Connecting the use of punishment with a lack of sufficient teacher know-how is a recurrent theme among stars.

The question of who is being punished for what must also be faced. Are offending students punishing themselves, other students, or the teacher? Teachers are frequently unaware of how some students push them to resort to punishments only to prove that the students can control the teacher's behavior. In a very real sense, eliciting punishments can be quite rewarding to many students. It takes the focus off learning and makes the issue one of control. Here the student must ultimately win since he or she cannot be coerced into anything if willing to bear the consequences. Many students derive satisfaction from yanking the punisher's chain.

It is also necessary to point out that stars use the class as a group to set norms of expected behavior. Discipline, in their rooms, is not a simple matter between the teacher and the offender. It is a matter of justice and equity between the individual and the rest of the class. The class is somehow disturbed or prevented from working. The class recognizes offenses and what must be done. The effective teacher is, in a very real sense, the representative of the group, i.e., the maintainer of reasonable order and working conditions for the entire group. This does not mean that the teacher uses the group to ostracize or further alienate youngsters who are very likely to be in need of greater group acceptance, support, or recognition. It does mean that the effective teacher knows that his or her role is sometimes one of implementing an agreed-upon group standard. Indeed, if left to their own devices, children will frequently advocate inappropriately severe consequences. The teacher is needed to mitigate such harsh "justice." Star teachers use the group as a restraining force but do not throw offenders to the mercy of the group. When children abused by poverty are suddenly given authority over others, there is frequently too little mercy. Star teachers prepare and educate their students for this role of making judgments about their own behavior and the behavior of peers. The opposite of teacher authoritarianism is not using children as vigilantes. It is a carefully established form of shared governance between the teacher and the class.

Homework

Star teachers do not assign homework in the traditional sense, i.e., "Do page 58 in the arithmetic book." They try to create assignments that youngsters are able to do independently and successfully. These assignments are frequently planned with the children and grow out of some class activity. Finishing a story they have started or completing a part of a project they are working on are examples. Often, such homework assignments place the child in the position of expert or explainer to—rather than someone in need of help from—a parent. This means that homework is carefully conceived and not simply assigned (Haberman 1992).

Typically, homework involves repetitive exercises that children cannot do independently and, in many cases, that their parents cannot help them with very well. This places the teacher in the superior position of making assignments to both the child and the parent. When teachers then complain that parents won't cooperate, they mean that parents won't follow instructions or complete assignments any better than their children. There is some confusion in this situation regarding precisely who is responsible for teaching what to whom. In most cases unsuccessful teachers are holding "uncooperative" parents responsible for not teaching the same lessons the teacher has been unable to teach during school hours.

This morass does not trap star teachers. Their homework is not a regular routine of drill. Each assignment is special and must pass the same tests of meaningfulness and relevance as in-class activities must.

Finally, homework is not checked—it is shared. It is the kind of activity and assignment that must not be coerced or enforced. The teacher's question, "Did you bring your homework?" is replaced by a concern for making time in class to share. There must be sufficient time for youngsters to show and explain to teachers and classmates what they have done.

Parent Bashing

Most teachers define "support from home" as parents helping their children with assigned homework or supporting some action of school discipline. Star teachers, on the other hand, describe parental support in terms of parents showing an interest in what their children do in school and providing them with basics such as privacy, safety, sleep, nutrition, and health care.

There are, of course, many who don't—or can't—provide these basics to their children. Some are overwhelmed by being adolescents themselves; others have never experienced any degree of school success. It is possible to find examples of horrible parents who hurt their children by direct action as well as by neglect. Star teachers are extremely aware of youngsters who may be subjected to abuse and violence. They make referrals and seek help from social workers or those in the criminal justice system. They are also more willing than many other teachers for the school to assume a broader role. Phrases such as "we can't be all things for all people" or "we can't be parents for these kids, too" are much less likely to be voiced by star teachers. A sense of shared responsibility characterizes stars' relationships with parents. They are more willing to call and to make home visits, even in unsafe neighborhoods. Their contacts with parents begin with establishing relationships and reporting positive things about children. When and if there are negative things to communicate, the groundwork has been laid for joint action.

During a recent study of failures and quitters, I interviewed a young teacher whose classroom consisted of three five-year-olds who had been placed in a special program for the emotionally disturbed. This teacher also had an aide. The school week was four days long, and Mondays were devoted to making home visits. When I asked this teacher her reason for quitting, she told me that the "parents don't care." Whenever the teacher visited a particular home, the parent kept watching television as the teacher spoke to her. No matter how many times the teacher asked, this parent would not make sure her son came to school with his glasses—and he was incapacitated without them. Ultimately, this teacher resigned and took a position in the suburbs (Haberman and Rickards 1990). I presented this problem to star teachers, who responded to the two issues as follows: "I would ask the parent to turn down the set and might even do so myself. More importantly, I would keep the child's glasses in school and let the parent worry about his having a pair at home." Stars generally laughed or shook off the possibility that this would be a reason for resigning a job with so few children, an aide, and one day per week to work with parents.

This example is the exception. Most parents do care, and care a great deal. They are frequently made to feel helpless by the ways in which schools and teachers present problems to them. In some cases they may feel denigrated by the way in which schools and teachers communicate, or the reasons for this communication.

Star teachers do not blame parents. As much as they may find out about the child and/or the family, they use the information as a basis for helping children learn more or want to learn more. Quitters and failures use what they find out to prove to themselves and to anyone who will listen that they cannot be held accountable for teaching children from such backgrounds. Historically, many teachers have "blamed the victim" by pointing to studies that showed students' inferior intelligence. This attribution freed the teacher from responsibility. When such reliance on heredity fell out of fashion, a newer, more sophisticated basis was needed in order to blame the victim and exonerate the schools. "Dysfunctional family" fills the bill. The undemocratic attribution of bad genes is now replaced by an apparent concern for a decent environment and a nurturing family. In either case it is a matter of blaming the victim. Effective teachers continue to believe that most parents care a great deal and, if approached in terms of what they can do, will be active, cooperative partners.

Tests and Grading

Star teachers spend as little time as possible on tests and grading. Apart from particular school rules that must be followed, they are generally quite disinterested in the topics. Their evaluations are based primarily on students' effort. They think in terms of specific tasks and accomplishments of their students, rather than in grades or general abstractions. Portfolios are much more in line with their proclivities and predispositions. They eschew competitive comparisons that are norm-referenced. For this reason, they have little faith in—and place little credence on—standardized tests of any kind.

Star teachers are interested in effort, not ability. They evaluate how involved their students become in a particular activity, and how hard they work on a project. They do not concern themselves with I.Q. measures, or other experts' assessments of ability. As a result, stars inevitably evaluate themselves whenever they assess student performance. Because they accept responsibility for interesting the students and engaging them in activities, they interpret student effort as an indicator of their own effectiveness as well as a measure of student output. How can the effective teacher separate student effort from his or her own ability to involve the student? Once the teacher uses effort as the primary indicator for assessing students' work, it is no longer possible to determine whether the teacher has failed or the student has failed. Typically, stars share the responsibility with those students who are not putting forth much effort. They examine their methods and seek better strategies for involving students in the future. This means that stars are also prone to attribute failing grades to themselves for students who have failed. Conversely, when students do well, stars attribute most of the success to students' hard work and little to themselves.

There is now a growing body of research to support what star teachers have always done. In attribution theory it is important to determine how the child explains success. Children who explain their failures on the basis of ability are prone to think less of themselves and to try less. If it's all a question of ability, one should succeed with little or no effort and, by third or fourth grade, most youngsters in poverty believe this to be the case. Thus, youngsters who make this attribution are left in an at-risk position at a very early stage of their school careers (Graham 1991). They quickly decide they can or cannot do a task, and do not persist. They come to view themselves as either smart or dumb. On the other hand, students who attribute their success or failure to effort can protect their self-esteem and hold on to some hope. After all, "If I had tried harder, I could have done it."

Star teachers understand this dynamic and teach their children to stress effort, rather than to believe in a static notion of ability. They know from experience, as well as from their ideology, that children, like adults, generally operate on only a small portion of their potential. They perceive marking and grading as merely a part of their total approach with children. They emphasize effort in order to keep youngsters involved in the system. I have never met a star teacher clutching a grade book, or averaging grades based on test scores, or taking papers home simply to grade them, or meeting with parents just to share grades, or using grades as the primary basis for recommending retention, or grouping children on the basis of grades, or complaining about grades, or happily entering grades on permanent records, or using grades to explain to a child how he or she was progressing.

Time-on-Task

Stars do not use direct instruction as their primary method and, therefore, do not see their role as monitoring students' time on task. Stars use some variation of the project method. They teach in units that frequently involve team or collaborative learning. Time-on-task is a concept for monitoring seatwork, homework, drill, practice of some isolated skill, or completion of a teacher-made assignment. Star teachers are extremely sensitive to the amount of time and effort students spend on tasks, but these are neither necessarily nor usually tasks simply assigned by the teacher. Stars do not think in terms of isolated or discrete tasks for which they must oversee student compliance. They develop tasks that are part of larger projects students are involved in planning. How much time students spend is an indicator of interest and involvement. It tells the star teacher when to try to generate more interest, or when to move on to something else. Star teachers begin by recognizing that the final power over learning is in the hands of the students. They regard themselves, rather than the children, as "on task" as long as they are seeking ways to involve students in learning activities. If anyone is to be judged by time on task, stars reserve this criterion for themselves. Doing clerical chores or complying with other requirements of the school bureaucracy drives them to distraction. They feel "off task" whenever they are not working on creating environments for learning, or interacting directly with students.

Rewards and Reinforcements

Securing compliance is not the way star teachers think about their jobs. They don't plan or use clever rewards such as stickers, smiling faces, or tickets for pizza and hamburgers. Their goal is to work toward intrinsic motivation and not to pretend that teachers can create a lifelong learner by endless—and largely meaning-less—payoffs. Stars are prone to give a child a book, or a model, or some material, but this is done on an individual basis and because they have identified a student's interest. Their gifts are not rewards, but an attempt to capitalize on a teachable moment—the times when a teacher breaks through to a student and finds an interest, talent, or goal. Given at these critical junctures, a book may spur future learning and support the child's efforts at becoming an independent learner.

In this chapter we have discussed not merely what star teachers do not do, but how they put a different spin on common teacher strategies. They discipline, but primarily through the learning activities they offer, and not as a detached prior condition. They don't punish but do, at times, use logical consequences so that youngsters learn to predict the effects of their behavior. They give homework but not traditional kinds. They work with parents, rather than supervise, inform, or blame them. They mark and grade as little as possible and shift the student's explanation of success from ability to effort. They are suspicious of direct instruction and do not regard time on task as their primary instructional strategy. It is more likely that they consider the time students spend on an activity as an indicator of their *own* ability to generate interest and of the children's need to be involved or to move on. Finally, because they reject the effectiveness of behavior modification in creating lifelong learners, they don't think in terms of rewards and reinforcements. Their goal is to move children off external rewards and onto making internal commitments; i.e., into learning stuff because they feel like it and because learning feels good. This concept is largely unheard of in most urban schools.

What Stars Think They're Doing

Star teachers conceive that their primary goal is turning kids on to learning—
i.e., engaging them in becoming independent learners. This doesn't mean that they
don't care about student learning, but they use learning as an opportunity to create
this higher goal of engagement. On the other hand, some teachers see the achievement of specific learning objectives, connected with future employment, as their
major purpose. The difference is not that one group values learning more than the
other, but star teachers see learning as a much broader goal.

Learning vs. Job Training

The subject of numerous education dissertations and articles has been "what
most U.S. citizens and most parents want their children to get out of 13 years of
schooling." Specific topics typically include:

- Basic skills and information.
- Principles and concepts of various subject matter areas.
- Skills in solving problems, making independent judgments, and thinking
  critically.
- Skills of group living and citizenship.
- Personal and environmental health.
- Aesthetic development.
- Character (development of personal values and ethics).
- Positive self-concept.
- Development of individual talents and abilities.
- Basic knowledge and skills for participating in the world of work.

These 10 goals may be ranked in various ways by the parents of suburban and
rural children, who comprise approximately 75 percent of the school population.
However, when parents or the public at large are asked to rank these goals for "other
people's children," i.e., for the 25 percent—or approximately 12 million predomi-
nantly poor and minority children—in urban schools, the list collapses down to two
objectives: basic skills and participation in the world of work. In simple terms, "Get

a job and stay out of jail." It is not an accident of history or chance that vocational high schools are in city school systems and not in suburban districts. Indeed, there has been a clear trend over the past century toward earlier identification of children who might be prepared for the world of work. In most urban districts, "career education," or "school-to-work," is now introduced as early as kindergarten. Increasingly, U.S. citizens are seeing great value in the European and Asian systems, which use grades and testing to decide at approximately age 11 which children will go into vocational training and which will continue with general liberal arts studies and enter the university. Such early screening and tracking is supported on several grounds. First, by helping youngsters see learning as a useful reason for going to or staying in school, it will prevent and even solve the problem of dropouts that occur among early adolescents. Second, it will raise the quality of education offered the brighter, college-bound youngsters: teachers will have classes of students who can do the work and there will be fewer troublemakers. Third, industry and government will be saved money by not having to provide initial training to entry-level workers. Students will graduate from high school ready to enter the workforce.

The softhearted and increasingly less popular side of this debate is as follows. Children mature and develop at different rates. Many children are late bloomers. Some people do not decide to go to college until after age 30. Many who attend universities as late adolescents (age 18 to 22) do not apply themselves fully to advanced study. Early adolescence is too early to determine the future life path of children and to set it into stone so that people will never be able to change direction and pursue higher education. Those who make this argument see early vocational tracking as the primary means for keeping children from low-income families in low-level jobs (Oakes 1992).

Whose Need to Learn What?

Star teachers have other, more fundamental reasons for maintaining their belief in all 10 goals, and avoid narrowing the school curriculum to basic skills and job readiness. They believe all youngsters should learn as much as they can from as broad and varied a curriculum as possible. Without using the jargon of academe, star teachers are avid proponents of the arts and sciences curriculum for all children. They know that children naturally come to school curious about, and interested in, science. Explanations of how the world works is their primary concern. At the same time, stars know that children begin as free and open artists ready to participate fully in every form of art. Stars not only believe that all children in poverty can learn, but that they should learn as much as possible in the widest possible range of subjects. The greatest arts and sciences faculty are not in the graduate schools of our most prestigious universities, but are star teachers in our slum elementary schools. These

teachers have children who are still largely uncontaminated by the misconception that the use of knowledge is to get a job or secure some extrinsic reward. Young children still see knowledge for what it is;

its primary functions are to answer life's most pressing questions and lead to further questions and more knowledge. Children begin school intrinsically motivated to learn as much as possible, because they sense in their bones that learning is synonymous with living and growing. It is only after children begin school and are forced to respond to teachers whose major objective is class discipline, and whose strongest emotion is fear that they might lose control of the class, that children are taught to do things for extrinsic rewards: stars, stickers, longer recess, certificates for pizza, etc. (Like countless others, my grandson began school knowing how to read and loving to do so. But in school, teachers began rewarding him for reading and effectively taught him that reading is only something you do for teachers if they give you pizza stamps.)

Unfortunately, most teachers are quite effective at transforming young children's interest in learning for its own sake into something teachers or others have to force you or bribe you to do. I believe most of this is done for two reasons. First, the assignments teachers give children are not made interesting. Second, the teacher's strategy for controlling and disciplining a class that he or she perceives might get out of hand at any time is some form of behavior modification. By giving or withholding rewards and implementing a system of punishments, teachers actually take intrinsically motivated children, who enjoy learning for its own sake, and transform them into game players. The game is played and learned over several years, but, by upper elementary and middle school, it might be called, "Try and Make Me."

Stars do not use behavior modification. They seek to keep children open to learning—in all forms—because learning has intrinsic validity. Stars' behavior never implies that "If you do this, I will like you, and if you don't, I won't." Such means of gaining children's compliance is just as extrinsic as the giving of other rewards unrelated to learning. Teachers and others with experience in urban schools are well aware of the fact that many—and in upper grades *most*—of the children have no sense of why they are there. These youth are keenly aware that the assignments that fill their hours, days, weeks, and months are not helping them with their problems of daily living. They also know that doing these assignments will not get them better jobs or, perhaps, any job at all. They do know that most teachers have given up trying to convince them of these reasons for doing their work and merely make assignments without trying to justify them. The few more caring teachers still try to convince students that their assignments will teach them useful things. These more caring teachers actually experience more failure than the teachers who have given up trying to justify their assignments. When students reject, ignore, or do not complete work assigned after the teacher has tried to justify it as useful, it is a clear indication of teacher failure. Teachers who simply make assignments are less likely to regard students' inadequate work as a failure on their part.

Star teachers hold an entirely different view of what they are doing. They are able, with painstaking effort that may take half the school year, to convince the children of their approach. Simply stated, it is that learning is good—it feels good, it is right, it is natural, it can be enjoyable, and it is what we do here. It is a natural act—like eating, sleeping, or breathing.

Stars get children to believe in the intrinsic value of learning because they believe in it themselves and are lifelong learners of various subjects, skills, and fields of study. Stars do not fall into the trap of trying to justify what children do all day by saying, "You'll need to know the capital of Wisconsin when you go for a job some-day." They regard such rationale as useless and counterproductive. Most teachers practice a system of external reinforcement for modifying children's behavior because they know of no other viable choices. Stars seek to convince their students that learning is itself the reward. They persist until their students also see learning as sufficient reason for being in school.

During a typical elementary school career, children complete thousands of assignments. Teachers have the option of assuming responsibility for managing and controlling the completion of these myriad assignments, often by connecting them to some extrinsic reward—perhaps a job?—in some unforeseeable future. It is a hopeless task and helps explain why most children of poverty do not know what they are doing in school. Star teachers utilize an easier approach, but one that requires teacher know-how and persistent commitment. They convince children that learning is intrinsically useful. Some of their strategies for accomplishing this include:

1. Knowing that their children are likely to come from other teachers and classrooms in which extrinsic rewards have been used as a carrot to gain compliance.

2. Knowing that it will take time to wean children back from this approach, and arouse their natural curiosity and interest in learning.

3. Beginning the year with some external rewards for class, group, and individual participation, but watching for children to become interested in particular activities.

4. Constantly seeking activities that will elicit children's interest and effort.

5. Using various materials, objects, and equipment to elicit children's interests, even to the extent of employing "gadgeterial seduction."

6. Using computers and information systems of all kinds to involve children.

7. Using the problems students face every day in their neighborhoods as the basis for learning activities.

8. Building on events in other classrooms and around the school to arouse students' interest.

9. Utilizing events reported in the media to heighten students' interest.

10. Capitalizing on children's interests in music, games, and popular heroes.

11. Elaborating on interesting events and people from their subject matter.

12. Recognizing that the outstanding talents of some children—such as singing, playing chess, programming computers, dancing, speaking another language, etc.—will spur the interests of others.

13. Modeling learning behavior by bringing their own interests to class: weaving, writing, construction, filmmaking, etc.

14. Using individual leaders, and the natural influence of groups and teams, to follow up activities.

15. Raising questions—the answers to which they do not know—that will

spark the curiosity of children and spur them to investigate and explain to the teacher.

16. Using real events—such as a performance for parents, a class magazine, or the production of a school play or program—as a focus for involving children.

17. Spending countless hours listening to children tell about their activities out of school, to learn what their interests and talents might be.

18. Meeting with parents to learn more about children's current and potential activities.

19. Conferring with other teachers, reading popular journals, and searching for new ideas and strategies that will interest children in activities.

20. Modeling behaviors that constantly demonstrate to the children that the teacher cares about and is trying to interest and involve them in activities.

Through these behaviors and numerous others, stars teach children that a naturally derived interest is the best basis for real learning. Even more, that learning can then take on a life of its own and proceed without direction from a teacher.

In the teacher-control option, the children are really in control while the teacher only appears to be accountable. Ultimately, students cannot be forced to learn, and the game of teachers pretending otherwise is one that traditional teachers inevitably lose. In the classroom climate established by stars, children come to share accountability and accept responsibility for what they learn. Learning is transformed from teacher assignments to "something we're in together." When this feeling begins to take hold, stars realize they have created islands and safe harbors for children against the popular culture of the school.

It should be clear from this analysis and the list of sample star behaviors that what stars know and believe about teaching is inextricably linked to their behaviors. Only behaviorists would impute isolated value to the behaviors themselves. To understand how stars function, it is necessary to understand how they think and what they believe, as well as the tasks they perform. Stars practice a craft derived from their ideology. This analysis cannot be summarized as "stars believe in learning as a natural act." To appreciate the finesse and commitment they demonstrate, it is necessary to first understand how the culture lived out in poverty schools actively works against what stars are seeking to accomplish—and actually do achieve.

The Functions of Star Teachers

In this chapter 15 functions of star teachers are described. To help in understanding these people, I have included some dialogue, as well as narrative description. The dialogue portions are composites from more than 1,000 interviews. The dialogue reveals the thinking of stars, and how their ideology differs from that of quitters and failures. The way stars think about their work cannot be separated from their observable behaviors. Their beliefs and behaviors reflect an integrated ideology. Their commitment to a number of "should be's" about the purpose of school and about teaching children in poverty forms an integrated whole. For these reasons, it is not possible to take what stars do and create "10 easy steps" for all other teachers to follow. To do what stars do requires sharing their commitment and ideology, because it is this foundation that guides the countless decisions they make daily. To try to imitate what stars do without believing as they do leads to merely going through the motions of teaching, and having little influence on students' learning. For those who accept stars' ideology, these functions are brought to life; they become a source of insight and a guide to effective action.

Persistence

The first function performed by star teachers is sometimes referred to as "problem solving." At times, it appears to be an indicator of creativity. Over the years I have come to regard it as "persistence," because it is inextricably linked to commitment. After listening to star teachers explain their work, I realize that this attribute does not reflect simple stubbornness. It reveals the deep and abiding beliefs that stars hold about the nature of children in poverty and their potential; the nature of stars' roles as teachers; and the reasons stars believe they and the children are in school.

Each of these functions represents a cluster of teacher behaviors *and* the ideology stars hold as a rationale for engaging in these behaviors. Thus, persistence represents both how stars act and what they believe.

As an ideology, persistence can best be described in the following manner.

Chapter 3

Stars believe that it is their responsibility to find ways of engaging their students in learning. Stars describe their jobs—to themselves as well as to others—as the continuous generation and maintenance of student interest and involvement. They believe that their ability to persist is manifested in several ways. First, for the class as a whole, they feel a constant responsibility to make the classroom an interesting, engaging climate that, on a daily basis, involves the children in all forms of learning. Second, on an individual level, stars are persistent in meeting the needs of the talented, those with handicapping conditions, and the frequently neglected "gray-area" kids. Stars verbalize their persistence like this: "There may be 30 kids in this class, but if I find an especially vital activity for one or two children today, I can reach everyone as an individual several times every month." This view of their role requires great persistence. The third way stars demonstrate this attribute is with problem children. The ultimate test in teaching is finding "what works." This is teacher talk for "Was the problem controlled?" or "Did the child with the problem get to work or stop bothering others?" "Finding what works" is a clear demonstration that teaching is a craft devoted to managing symptoms—not deep-seated causes or bases for children's actions. Whatever the reason for children's behavior—whether poverty, personality, a handicapping condition, a dysfunctional home, or an abusive environment—classroom teachers are responsible for managing children, seeing that they work together in a confined space for long periods, and ensuring that they learn.

The following two conversations illustrate stars' persistence in thought and action. The first dialogue is with a low-potential teacher on his or her way to quitting or failing. In contrast, the second conversation is with a star. As you read, focus on the attribute of persistence.

Conversation #1

Setting:	**Third/fourth grade**
Problem:	**Child does not do homework**
Questioner:	Imagine that, when you start school next September, you have a youngster who doesn't do his homework. Several days go by, and this behavior continues. What might you do?
Teacher #1:	I'd want to find out why the child was not doing his homework. There could be many, many reasons. Some children don't do homework because they don't have a place to work. Others just lose stuff on the way home.

Questioner: What might you do about this problem? Franklin hasn't done his homework for several days now.

Teacher #1: I'd try to find out why.

Questioner: You'd talk to him?

Teacher #1: Yes, I'd talk to him.

Questioner: Would you speak to him in front of the class, or privately? What would you say to him?

Teacher #1: I'd probably talk with him privately. I'd try to find out what was going on. Maybe offer to help him.

Questioner: Suppose having this private conference works. Franklin brings in his homework for the next two days. On the third day there's no homework. What might you do now?

Teacher #1: I'd talk to him again. Maybe try to encourage him with a reward of some sort.

Questioner: Suppose this works for another few days and Franklin does some homework. But then he stops. What might you do then?

Teacher #1: Well, speaking to him several times, I'd also mention some consequences if he doesn't do his work.

Questioner: Like what?

Teacher #1: Oh, perhaps withdrawing a privilege . . . something he enjoys, like recess.

Questioner: Now you've spoken with him several times, you've given some rewards and withdrawn some privileges, and Franklin still doesn't do his homework. What might you do now?

Teacher #1: By this time I would probably call a parent, perhaps discuss the situation with his mother.

Questioner: O.K. Let's imagine that this too works, but only for a few days. After that Franklin is back to his old ways . . . no homework. What might you do now?

Teacher #1: Well, by this time the problem has been going on for some time. I might take the matter up with the school psychologist and have Franklin tested. There might be something wrong with him.

Questioner: That's certainly true. But the school psychologist has a backlog of children to test. It might take five or six months. Is there anything else you might do?

Teacher #1: At this point I might ask the principal for help. Maybe a three-way

Chapter 3

Questioner: meeting with the mother.
And Franklin?

Teacher #1:   Maybe, sure!

Questioner: I know you're getting tired of this same question, but I have to ask one more time. Franklin still is not handing in his homework. What might you do at this point?

Teacher #1:   At this point, it's clear that there's something seriously wrong with Franklin. I don't know. (Pause) It's tough. (Pause) I might ask to have Franklin put in another classroom.

Questioner: O.K. Let's pull away from Franklin and no homework. Let's look at the whole job of teaching this class. Think about all the tasks: teaching, managing, everything else. Imagine the whole responsibility for all 30 children's learning. How often do you ask the question, "I wonder what I do next?"

Teacher #1:   "I wonder what I do next?"

Questioner: That's right but, not just in relation to kids with a problem, in relation to everything you have to do.

Teacher #1:   Well, a lot I would guess, now that I think about it.

Questioner: Once a year, once a month, once a week—"I wonder what I do next?"

Teacher #1:   Well, I think it's important to be well planned. If you're well planned and there aren't any Franklins. . . .

Questioner: Assume things are going well. How often would you ask yourself this question?

Teacher #1:   Oh, I would guess then it might not be so necessary. . . . Maybe once a month, maybe once every couple of weeks. I'm not sure.

The following conversation involves the same questions, raised with a star teacher.

Conversation #2

Setting: **Third/fourth grade**

Problem: **Child does not do homework**

Questioner: Imagine that, when you start school next September, you have a youngster who doesn't do his homework. Several days go by, and this behavior continues. What might you do?

Teacher #2:   I probably wouldn't wait a couple of days.

Questioner: All right, let's assume it was the first day. What would you do?

Teacher #2: I'd take the child aside privately and try to find out what the problem was. Did he understand the assignment? Did he want to do it? Why? Why not? Maybe there's some other problem that's getting in the way of homework.

Questioner: O.K. So you'd speak with the child. Suppose that didn't work. What now?

Teacher #2: I'd be likely to look for something that seemed to interest him and make up a special assignment for him.

Questioner: So you'd give him something special to do?

Teacher #2: Something that I knew he could do and wanted to.

Questioner: O.K. Let's imagine that you went to all this trouble, made up a special assignment for him, and he still didn't do it.

Teacher #2: Well, I'd want to check out what might be preventing him.

Questioner: What would you do?

Teacher #2: Would it be all right if I gave more than one answer at a time?

Questioner: Sure.

Teacher #2: I'd probably chat with the teachers who had him previously and see if they had this problem. I might ask another adult in the school to speak with him for the purpose of finding out what's going on. Eight- and nine-year-olds who know they've done something "wrong" aren't always very revealing. I might check the school records. I might call a parent. I might find out who in the class was his friend, and see what they could tell me about his interests and talents. He might have a brother or sister in another class that could be helpful. Perhaps an aide or paraprofessional has worked with him and could give me some insights. I might visit his home if the matter persisted over time.

Questioner: You've mentioned seven or eight things. I notice you haven't spoken with the principal or the school psychologist.

Teacher #2: I might speak with the principal, but I'm assuming no homework is my problem, not a cause for suspension or something. I haven't spoken with the school psychologist for several reasons. First, they test and then always say, "This child might be helped by more individual attention." Heck, all children might be helped by more individual attention. Second, I'm not looking to have a child put in a special class because his crime is no homework. So far that's all you've said he's done—or not done.

Chapter 3

Questioner: O.K. So now we know a bunch of things you would do and a few you would not. Franklin still doesn't do his homework.

Teacher #2: I'd keep talking to him. I'd keep trying to find things he could do successfully without having to take many materials back and forth between home and school.

Questioner: You're back on the action you tried at the beginning.

Teacher #2: That's right. Talking with children is my job. So's trying to find things they can do and will do.

Questioner: You do the same things that don't work—over and over?

Teacher #2: They do work. I'm pretty sure this problem would have been solved a long time ago. You keep stating it's not working. Children don't resist doing things they care about—particularly with teachers and other students who show an interest. That's another thing I would do. Create an expectation from me and from other children in the class who are interested in learning that we all want to hear about the particular assignment Franklin has done for homework.

Questioner: We've spent a lot of time on this. . . .

Teacher #2: Don't be concerned; we'll work it out with Franklin.

Questioner: O.K. Let's pull away from this homework issue. I'd like to get some overall sense from you about how often you ask yourself this question, "I wonder what I do next?"

Teacher #2: "I wonder what I do next?"

Questioner: Yes, but not in relation to discipline or problems—in relation to your total work as a teacher, as you look at your total work in the classroom. Whether it's learning, managing, or whatever, how often would you ask yourself, "I wonder what I do next?"

Teacher #2: A lot would depend on the class. . . .

Questioner: Let's assume things are going well. There are no problems.

Teacher #2: There are never "no problems." But whatever you mean, I can tell you that I ask myself this question all the time.

Questioner: Once a month? Once a week? Once a day?

Teacher #2: All the time. Every day. Countless times each day. Even when things seem to be going well, the children could be learning more, I could be finding more ways of involving them and eliciting greater activity and learning from them. Since I can never engage them enough in learning, I can never stop finding a better way. I can imagine asking a question like "What do I do next?" for the class, for a group, for one child—20 times a day.

As we contrast the answers of Teacher #1 and Teacher #2, several clear differences emerge. Teacher #1 perceives the issue as a problem that should not occur, while Teacher #2 perceives the problem as part of his or her regular, normal workload. Teacher #1 perceives the problem as something to be dealt with through a series of rewards and punishments. Teacher #2 does not define the issue as involving rewards and punishments, but as a search for an activity that will gain the child's interest. Teacher #1 perceives him- or herself as an authority in search of a surefire method of forcing compliance. Teacher #2 conceives of the teacher's role less as an authority and more as a skilled practitioner, charged with involving the child in learning. Teacher #1 seeks support and backup from the principal and school psychologist. Teacher #2 sees these roles as of little potential value— unless they happen to know the child personally and have some way of involving him in learning. This seems an unlikely possibility to Teacher #2.

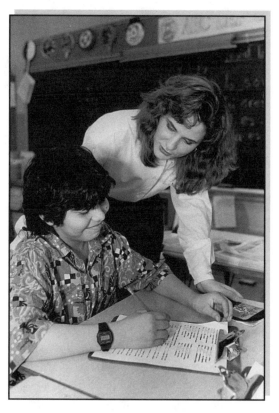

Teacher #1 sees relating to parents as helping to force compliance. Teacher #2 is loathe to involve the mother but would approach her with the same problem the teacher faces: Is there something the child is interested in or good at? Teacher #1 sees a final solution: either the child will comply or be taken out of the room. Teacher #2 sees the possibility that the issue will be ongoing. It may be solved temporarily, but will crop up again. Teacher #2 is expecting to resolve the issue, but is also open to the possibility that he or she may have to revisit the issue again at

Chapter 3

some future time. This doesn't seem to upset Teacher #2, who appears to define the main task of a teacher as finding things that will involve children in learning. The attitude Teacher #2 conveys—it can be verbalized in various ways—is something like this: "If teaching were simply a question of giving children assignments then trying to force compliance, anybody off the street could be a teacher. The knowledge we need teachers to bring into the classroom is how to elicit interest and engage youngsters in wanting to do the work of learning. It may seem harder, but I can tell you that working with volunteers is a lot easier than overseeing prisoners."

The second question, "How often do teachers ask themselves 'What do I do next?'" also highlights differences between the two teachers. Teacher #1 perceives the question to be a reasonable one only if there are no "problems." When the question was amplified to, "In a class that's working well, how often would you ask yourself this question?" Teacher #1 could not really see a need for it. This is because Teacher #1 does not define his or her role as one of constantly searching for more effective ways of involving children. Also, Teacher #1 does not define his or her job as open-ended; one of encouraging children to do more, learn more, be more. Teacher #1 sees teaching as essentially managing. If there are no problems—i.e., threats to the teacher's authority—then there is no need to be concerned. Teacher #1's motto might well be, "If it ain't broke, don't fix it!"

In contrast, Teacher #2 is constantly trying to make things better. He or she sees endless potential beyond compliance, and knows that all students can always be learning more. Teacher #2 feels and acts accountable for involving the children in more and more. Because Teacher #2 cannot conceive of learning as a finite task, he or she persists and persists and persists. This behavior is a combination of his or her ideology *and* a series of behaviors. In truth, Teacher #2's (and all stars') persistent behaviors comprise their day-to-day work. They will persist until they find meaningful work for every child in the classroom. And if, by some miracle, they have linked every child in the class with a useful learning activity, they will continue to persist by asking themselves, "Is this the very best activity that can be devised, or might there be something even better for students to be doing?" Stars think in terms of maximum—not minimum—standards.

For star teachers, persistence is not merely a behavior or a set of behaviors. It is also a clear reflection of what they believe the daily work of the teacher to be. A quote attributed to Thomas A. Edison states, "The difference between coal and diamonds is that diamonds stayed on the job longer."

Protecting Learners and Learning

For star teachers, the ultimate value to be preserved is learning. For quitters and failures, it is order. Stars live this belief by constantly seeking out and capitalizing on problems, questions, discrepant events, current crises, and emergencies. They bring these into the classroom and use them to involve students in learning—and going beyond—traditional textbook curricula. Stars' sources are twofold: they are alert and sensitive to current events that might capture the imagination of children, and they have their own interests and avocations that they share with the children. Examples of the former are usually one-time or short-term topics, such as a heroic dog saves a child who has fallen into a river, a local hero makes a hit record, or the controversy about where to dump chemical waste. Such issues provide food for thought, analysis, discussion, and problem solving. Children are involved in reading, writing, debating, and thinking about the particular issue. Star teachers use these "hot topics" as vehicles for bringing to life concepts in science, math, and language and making them meaningful to children. Topics such as "the spread of disease" or "property rights as a constitutional guarantee" are in the rooms of typical teachers, "covered" by reading a series of abstractions with little or no relevance to students' lives. When stars use organizing themes such as "the chemical waste in my neighborhood and how it might cause specific diseases and other problems" or "who has the right to tell people where to dump stuff and why," then concepts regarded as largely irrelevant suddenly take on personal meaning. Taught in these personal ways, grand ideas and ideals can be learned and remembered by even the youngest children. Unfortunately, teachers without sufficient knowledge of basic science, math, language, or social studies do not know these concepts and can only follow along in textbooks. Stars use texts while texts use failure teachers.

What this means in day-to-day practice is that the actual work of teaching and learning—what is discussed, written about, read, the actual activities in classrooms—is entirely different in the rooms of stars and in the rooms of other teachers. In the rooms of failures, one sees a clear pattern of "Take out your math books and turn to page 58." "It's ten thirty and time for science. Take out your books and open to Chapter 3. Who hasn't read yet?" "Open your *American People* to page 164. Now yesterday we left the Pilgrims meeting Squanto. . . ." What a classroom observer witnesses are teachers reading the text to children, perhaps stopping to explain. More likely, the teacher will use a set of prepared questions from the teacher's guide to ask questions at appropriate points. Another likely scenario is that the children will take turns reading the text aloud and the teacher will interject with questions or elaborations. Another common practice is for children to read the material silently and answer the questions at the end of the chapter in writing. The teacher then repeats the questions and calls on children to read aloud the answers they have written. Sometimes there's a test, and children exchange their papers. Another possibility is that the teacher has taken a workshop in cooperative learning. The class may then be divided into groups or teams who answer a set of questions as a group, thereby enabling peers to help each other. Children spend five or six hours a day for 13 years and emerge not only semiliterate and largely ignorant but without any commitment to learning. They have never experienced the joys of learning.

In these ways teachers "cover" the material in textbooks. Publishers sell the texts or "packages" to administrators and school boards as teacher-proof programs rather than as sets of books. In addition to the books themselves, there are teacher guides, pictures, a bibliography of supplementary materials, and tests. The whole package is premised and sold on the notion that the teacher may be ignorant or disinterested in the material he or she is teaching but that, by following the teacher's guide, he or she can effectively teach it, even to reluctant learners.

Supporting the premise that you can teach what you don't know or particularly care about are the patterns of how teachers typically cover textbook material. The teacher is usually a better reader than the children. The teacher also has the teacher's guide and the answers to the questions. The elementary teacher, as a more experienced older adult and a college graduate, is likely—but not necessarily—to have a broader information base (not basic knowledge) about the subjects. With this edge, teachers who don't know why it rains, or how the earth was formed, teach science. Using their skills of reading, perhaps a chapter or paragraph ahead of the class, teachers who don't know what's in the Constitution teach children about being good citizens. Untroubled by ignorance, teachers with no understanding of concepts such as zero, infinity, sets, or symbolic language teach arithmetic. Indeed, we have substantial evidence that many elementary teachers are not only limited or ignorant of the subjects they teach, they are actually casualties and college failures of these studies, particularly subjects such as math, science, foreign language, music, and dance. In most states that require a written test of basic skills for teacher certification, the level of passing is set at about eighth grade, which is the same passing level set for the GED high school equivalency diploma. The typical teacher-preparing institution requires one course in general math for future teachers, and two or three low-level courses in science. Any passing grade will qualify an individual for a teaching license (Haberman in press).

Most of those who choose elementary education as a college major do so because (1) they "love children" and (2) they believe they can meet the general education requirements of the school of education. In discussing their perceptions of what they must learn to teach children, they generally focus on methods of teaching and the practice of student teaching. They believe they can teach reading—not because they know literature, language, and writing and because they engage in these processes with a passion—but because they know how to read. The reading methods courses they take will, they believe, enable them to teach children to read (Haberman and Glassner 1995). Nowhere in the state or university requirements is it mandated that a future teacher be an avid student of literature, or writing, or language. The assumption is that, if one is able to read at a particular grade level and takes courses in how to teach reading, this is sufficient. The criticism that future elementary teachers don't know ethnic writers or female writers is certainly true, but trivial. The assertion that they know few, if any, U.S. writers—living or dead—is more serious, and also generally true.

A similar student perception exists regarding math. If one can add or subtract numbers through 100, it is assumed that one can teach arithmetic in first grade. After all, the children can't do it! And so it goes with all the subject areas. Future teachers do not believe they need to know where subject-matter study leads, or how it developed, or how the key concepts of any subject can be effectively taught to young children. Future teachers believe that all they must know is how to do the exact assignments they give children in order to teach them those subjects (Haberman 1986b). This is not merely a misperception but a hoax of monstrous proportions. It substitutes literacy—the ability to follow a teacher's guide or read a text—for the essential knowledge needed to teach various subject matters. Worst of all, it permits—even recruits—into the teaching profession individuals who have never experienced the joys of learning, learning for the sake of learning, the pursuit of a subject in depth because one has become addicted to it, the well-being that is unique to the knowledgeable learner, the sense of accomplishment that comes from hard study and application to a field, and most of all, the endless questions that pursue and tempt the individual who has learned enough to ask.

This might appear to be the age-old liberal arts and science criticism of teachers and teacher education, but it is exceedingly more complex. The reason that we can no longer abide teacher ignorance relates most directly to equalizing educational opportunity for children in poverty. The best way to define educational disadvantage is to think of it in the following way. To the extent that a child is dependent on schools and teachers for what he or she learns, the child is at an educational disadvantage. The reasons for this have been discussed earlier: schools sort by, track according to, and exacerbate the deficits with which children begin school; middle-class children have access to a wide array of learning resources and human resources outside of school, which are frequently more potent than those within school.

Children in poverty are less likely to have out-of-school models who are practicing chemists, language interpreters, writers, or others who can serve as models of knowledgeable people who derive great well-being as lifelong students of various disciplines. I am not referring here merely to occupations and professions (i.e., lawyers, doctors, accountants, etc.), but to the daily experience of interacting with adults who study and learn because they are well-educated, enthusiastic students of subjects from which they derive personal—not monetary or tangible—benefit. These are people who are intrinsically moved to be lifelong learners and who need no extrinsic reward to learn more about music, botany, philately, computer technology, or fish breeding. Children in poverty rarely, if ever, see such people, even on television.

Why is this important? What has it to do with teaching children in poverty? Everything! The elementary teacher who tries to motivate children by telling them, "You will need to know this someday to fill out an application form to get a job" or "You need to know this to make change at the grocery" is dead in the water as a generator of interest. Such reasons do not validate five hours of daily lessons over a six-year (K–5) elementary career. The teacher who pursues this method will end up repeating the same, stale half-dozen extrinsic motives for learning literally thousands of discrete lessons. It does not and will not work. Young children—and even adolescents—are not turned on to learning by the notion of future employment. They also sense that these teacher reasons are apocryphal. If poor people all read on grade level, there would still not be enough good jobs to go around. How can a job be used to rationalize learning something about Andrew Jackson, the rivers of California, or the distinction in the usage of *that* and *which* in the fourth grade? Exhortation by elementary teachers who seek to make learning relevant to children's future occupational lives will not work because it cannot be done. On the other hand, children's learning can be made relevant to their present lives, but that takes teachers who know sufficient subject matter to connect it with children's daily lives and real problems.

Where does this leave us? If their daily lessons can't be rationalized in terms of a future job—or at least staying out of jail—how are teachers to interest and engage children in learning? Star teachers know their only hope is to imbue the children's studies with intrinsic value. In truth, there is no other valid reason that can be given to children, over and over each day. True, the subjects taught in elementary school all have instrumental value, but not for jobs alone. They are means for becoming better citizens, and more fully actualized individuals. But to endlessly repeat these truisms to children is of no motivational use, and will have the reverse effect. If the reason for constant study cannot be, "You'll need this for a job someday," how do stars engage children in learning? They recognize that children can and will be naturally "turned on" to learning—not because it is always fun, but because it meets an abiding human need. All children *begin* school in love with learning; most have their curiosities squelched later on. As kindergartners, they are already convinced that knowledge is power, although they cannot verbalize this effect. They begin knowing the joys of learning, and they express and show their feelings. Stars try to keep this preschool flame lit and, in those for whom it has been dampened, to rekindle it. They know the children will readily accept pursuing activities because they choose to, or derive a sense of satisfaction from the subject or activity itself.

How do stars drop the pretense of some future utilitarian good, and deal honestly—and successfully—with children? How do stars communicate the idea that, "We do this because we learn a lot of good stuff"? Indeed, this learning has been so effectively gained and internalized that children in the classrooms of stars very seldom raise the question of why they need to study a subject. And if the children have been involved in the planning and selection of their activities, "very seldom" becomes "never."

The answer is clear and straightforward. Stars interest their children in learning by modeling their own interest in learning. At various and numerous times, stars read books, write stories, compose pictures, build things, conduct experiments, and engage in the full range of learning behaviors in the presence of their students. Their children see their teacher as a lifelong student of subjects and pursuits; an individual with enthusiasm and passion for learning things in great depth. By identifying with their teacher—through rapport, caring, mutual respect—children are naturally drawn to explore and sample the teacher's interests and pursuits. And in those cases where the children can share the teacher's interests, there is a happy and productive relationship. But even in instances in which the youngsters do not come to share the teacher's particular interests, the teacher has still exerted a profound and salutary influence on the children. He or she has demonstrated and modeled the behaviors of an intrinsically motivated learner. Even the children who do not come to share the teacher's particular passions will still be shown and taught, by example, to develop their own interests and studies. It takes a teacher who is him- or herself a learner to develop learners. This is the essence of the need for elementary as well as secondary teachers to be knowledgeable in the various subjects they teach. The usual argument of the arts and sciences advocates (you can't teach what you don't know) is correct but does not go far enough. Teachers' most powerful method—the actual means by which they can effectively teach children—is one of modeling. It takes a learner involved in something to teach the behaviors and satisfactions of intrinsic learning to others. This modeling is the primary means by which stars teach low-income children. One can frequently observe them engaging in a personal interest or study in front of and with their children. One does not hear them denigrate the value of their learning as, "You'll need this for a job someday."

Public school curriculum is very close to the general liberal studies of most university curricula. It includes a variety of ways to study social science, physical science, the arts, and humanities. Like liberal and general studies in the university, the primary purpose for learning these subjects is not vocational.

Thus far, I have attempted to show that, because modeling is the best way to foster children's intrinsic need to learn, teachers must themselves be active lifelong learners. I have also argued that giving artificial reasons such as an occupational need for engaging in liberal studies is not effective with children of any age. There is a third dimension that also differentiates star teachers from others. It is, as is true of all the star attributes, a combination of their ideology and their functioning. It is their commitment to some field of knowledge, or way of knowing, or subject matter as a guide to the way they think and act with children. They see knowing things and being able to do things as their ultimate goals for children. Whenever a star "hooks" a child on pursuing a subject or activity, he or she regards it as having hit a home run. In contrast, quitters and failures see effectively maintaining order as hitting a home run. Everything discussed heretofore is background for understanding the ideology and practice of protecting learners and learning.

Star teachers find projects that interest children. They then plan with children how they will set about studying the topics. Usually the projects are built around a set of questions or problems that are of vital interest to the children. Other times the project involves achieving a goal the children have decided upon. Inevitably, star teachers draw upon their own expertise and interests to guide children into fashioning these class projects. Following are a few examples of how stars accomplish this.

1. A teacher with knowledge of computers and music has adapted a program so that the children in her class can create their own music, fully scored, by composing and harmonizing even the simplest melody. The children begin to write poems and rap to their music. They soon compose so much that they decide to put on a class opera that depicts their

lives in and out of school. The class improves its reading and writing skills markedly. They learn more music, including some advanced skills of composition. They learn computer uses. They improve their oral language. Incidental learnings involve their ability to work more cooperatively and to persist in long-term tasks that require a month of continuous effort.

2. A teacher with an interest in botany regularly brings in plants. Soon the room is not big enough to hold them, and the class is given a plot that is part of an urban garden in what was formerly a vacant lot near the school. The children become interested in growing vegetables and in the related problems of protecting the plot from humans and neighborhood animals. The children, who represent diverse ethnic groups, are interested in vegetables commonly consumed by Asian-Americans. The shortened growing season requires that some seeds be started indoors. A summer project with volunteer gardeners is also necessary. Individual children, as well as the teacher, grow independent and team gardens near various people's homes. Some parents are involved. Learnings far exceed what is typical in a low-income urban school. While botany is the main study, children learn about weather, urban pollution, and lead in the soil. The project leads to subsequent investigations of urban health hazards, nutrition, and health.

3. An elementary teacher with knowledge and interest in psychology secures an old lie detector at public auction. These devices assess a respondent's veracity by measuring perspiration on the surface of the skin. The children become enthralled by the process of measuring lying. They speak and write endless scenarios as they take turns trying to assess each other's ability to lie. In addition to enhancing speaking, writing, and thinking skills, the teacher and children become fascinated with the question of why people perspire when they lie. A few children even become interested in some advanced concepts of science. When a person fools the machine, they demand, "Make him do it again!" (reliability). Other children raise issues of how we can really be certain that an individual is sweating because he's lying, and not because he's hot (validity). The project leads to a subsequent study of lying, various types of lies (are there ever any good lies?), and why people lie. The teacher's knowledge and interest of psychology encouraged these studies. Her enthusiasm for learning along with the children served as a model of the intrinsic learner.

4. A teacher who knows some anthropology brings a shortwave radio to class. The children begin listening to foreign broadcasts. The teacher picks up news, music, and even some children's programs. The children become interested in the English-language broadcasts originating from all of the continents and even from remote places around the world. They begin a project on the different ways people who use English speak. They become more sensitive not only to international differences but to the differences represented by the diverse backgrounds in their classroom. Using the radio broadcasts and themselves as examples, they begin to collect and compile in a computer program the various ways different people say the same things. Standard forms, vernacular, different usages, and Black English become continuous sources of comparison and learning. The project culminates with a series of stories and poems from a variety of English-speaking sources: Australia, the Caribbean, the U.S. South, U.S. urban areas, India, Scotland, Ireland, etc. The children not only improve their standard English forms but engage in genuine linguistic analyses of different culture groups.

These—and numerous other—examples can be gleaned from the stars' teaching. They are themselves avid learners who bring some form of expertise to their work and then model their love of learning for the children. By modeling such involvement with learning, the teacher makes intrinsic learning a reality in the lives of the children.

Why should this discussion elaborating the need to have knowledgeable lifelong learners as teachers be included in a section entitled "Protecting Learners and Learning"? The answer to this question brings us back to the function I wish to describe. It was first necessary, however, to establish the teacher as a lifelong student.

Star teachers achieve real learning in low-income schools by the project method exemplified by the four preceding examples. These examples are truly countless, since stars pursue such projects throughout their careers. But here the story takes a confrontational twist and reveals the manner in which stars implement this function.

Typical schools are not conducive to teachers' use of the project method described here. Schools are usually organized to meet state mandates that particular subjects be taught for a certain number of minutes per day and week to children in the various grade levels. Where states do not have such narrow, prescriptive regulations, local school systems do. This rigidity is intensified by the practice of requiring specific texts for each grade level, and expecting teachers to "cover" them. It is exacerbated by schools of education that advise future teachers to use direct instruction, and extrinsic rewards as motivation. As a result, the projects of star teachers are quite likely to be regarded in most schools, and by most principals and other teachers, as outside the regular curriculum. Indeed, this is typically the case. Stars constantly report that their day-to-day teaching (i.e., the project method described) is frequently resented by other teachers, or actually forbidden by school administrators. Stars explain, at great length and in exhaustive detail, the strategies they employ to retain their freedom to teach using the project method. In most cases their teacher colleagues come to feel less threatened when they realize that stars only want to be left alone and not necessarily to make others teach the project method. Many teachers are ill equipped to offer anything but direct instruction because they are not lifelong learners committed to the study of anything they can share and model with children. By various strategies, stars convince their colleagues they will not be "shown up" or threatened in any way if they are permitted the freedom to teach using the project method rather than direct instruction.

The approach with principals is a little different. Stars must convince their principals that the children's test scores will not go down and will, indeed, increase. They must also convince their principals that the benefits are worth the extra field trips, the additional equipment and unusual materials, the use of resource people, and the noise created by productive children.

It is no accident that stars generally have special agreements with school janitors. Their use of space, their need for extra equipment, and their inevitably

Chapter 3

greater production of refuse require janitors to do more work and to treat their classrooms differently.

The way this question plays out for many stars is as follows: "After I turn the class on to learning 'X', how do I protect them from the school bureaucracy?" The projects that stars use to engage children in learning are frequently perceived by rigid supervisors or principals as activities that must be stopped. (The four preceding examples are mild in comparison to others undertaken by stars and their children.) At other times, the projects conflict with school rules, bus schedules, or the use of space or equipment shared with other teachers. Frequently, other teachers who may feel threatened by the stars' projects denigrate and downgrade them to principals, who come to believe that stars just cause trouble. "Why can't they just teach like everyone else and be more 'cooperative'?"

For these and other perceived abuses, stars are frequently prevented from pursuing projects. This deterrence sometimes comes in the form of the principal saying, "I don't want your class to be doing X, Y, Z." This directness is most often true in the case of younger stars or newer principals. Frequently, the desist orders are more indirect, e.g., school rules don't permit certain activities; or curriculum requirements are stated in terms of the number of hours that must be spent in direct study of particular subjects; or school insurance doesn't cover certain activities. In one way or another, stars must frequently choose between an activity that their children really enjoy and are learning from, and complying with some school authority seeking to prevent the work from proceeding. Stars always choose the children over the system. They try negotiation and reasoning, and to prove that their children are learning from the activities. They collect portfolios. They invite skeptical principals and others to visit. They willingly submit to having their children tested to show that they are learning as much or more than children being taught by typical textbook instruction. Stars are also willing to move some of their time on projects to before school, after school, free time, weekends, and vacation periods. What they are not willing to compromise is the learning of their children. Because the stars' primary goal is to find projects that engage their children in real learning, they are unwilling to simply give up these powerful learning activities because colleagues or superiors do not appreciate them, or find them inconvenient to have around. At the same time, stars are not confrontational. They seek to negotiate with a principal who is trying to shut down one of their projects. They are unlikely to cause confrontations, start legal actions, or initiate union grievances.

Consider the following problem: A star's class is engaged in a project to which a principal objects. The principal's objection might be based on the belief that the star is not "covering" the traditional curriculum. The principal also might not like the extra noise, equipment, cleanup, or smells emanating from the star's classroom. The principal tells the star to stop the project and go back to the regular curriculum, i.e., use direct instruction to "cover" the textbook. At this point the issue is clear: a genuine learning activity that is teaching children at an advanced level and on which the children are thriving vs. compliance with the school rules, policies, and/ or principal's directive. Quitter and failure teachers don't regard this as a dilemma. If they were conducting a project to which the principal objects (unlikely), they would simply desist. They explain this behavior by saying, "The principal runs the school," or "The principal is the boss." When prompted and reminded that the children are learning and love the project, they typically respond, "I'm not about to get fired," or "The principal is accountable for what happens in the school." Other quitters and failures immediately go to the other extreme and become confrontational: "No one is going to tell me what to do!" or "I'll go to the union (superintendent) (parents) (school board)."

Stars, on the other hand, have two clear goals and persist toward them. First, if the children are deeply involved in a valuable learning activity, it is the teacher's job to keep it going. Second, it is their job to patiently, courteously, and professionally persist and negotiate with the principal. Quitters and failures offer quick and extreme solutions. Either they drop the project at the principal's first request, or immediately move to some sort of confrontation. Stars, in contrast, might persist in the following ways: have a conference with the principal; ask the principal to visit the classroom; meet again with the principal; collect data to show that the children are learning more than by traditional methods; collect samples of the children's work; meet again with the principal; have children and/or teachers from other classes observe the project; prepare a presentation (e.g., play, videotape, book, experiment, musical) that explains what the children are learning; meet with the principal again. Stars perceive themselves as the grease between the children and any school rule or policy that would grind them down. In the final analysis, if they were directly ordered to drop a project, they would still figure out a way to do it before or after school or on their own time. Stars would never give up an activity that excites children and leads to genuine learning.

Interestingly, when asked, "What would you tell the children if you stopped a project they cared about?" the quitters and failures respond that they would tell the children that the principal is making them stop. The very teachers who obey the

Chapter 3

principal's orders to stop are inevitably the ones who would lay the blame on him or her. Stars, on the other hand, who might be negotiating persistently with a school principal over many months to change his or her mind, would never tell their children that the principal is trying to stop their project. Stars are sufficiently sensitive that they do not want the principal to lose stature in the eyes of the children. They are also willing to take the heat for a decision they are fighting against. They want the children to see them as decision makers and not merely people who must follow orders.

This is a critical point, especially in schools serving low-income children. These children and their families are constantly abused or mistreated by bureaucracies such as the welfare department, health providers, housing authorities, insurance companies, the criminal justice system, utilities, etc. Children in poverty do not need to learn to believe that their school is just another selfish bureaucracy that claims to be helping them but is really run for its own convenience.

For children in poverty, succeeding in school is a matter of life and death. They cannot be rock stars or players in the NBA. They must make it in school or spend their lives in hopelessness and desperation. Children in poverty have no family resources or networks to help them start careers or businesses; they must succeed in school to have any hope of occupational mobility. Teachers should not lead poverty students to believe that schools are just like all the other bureaucracies; that schools could be both the agency that gets them involved in learning, and the one that makes them stop. Stars are sensitive to this, and will protect the school principal and stick up for school rules and policies even when it is exceedingly hard to do so. Stars' sensitivity to this point is still another reflection of their ideology. They know that they must get students to believe in schools even if there are particular things about school that sometimes don't work. Stars know that everything about life in school is educative—not just the formal lessons. As a result, should they be required to stop or change a project that students like, they will take personal responsibility for this decision, and plan for other ways to continue the project, rather than lead students to lose faith in the school.

Quitters and failures are sensitive to none of this. Not having thought about the issue, they assume the goal of the school, particularly for children in poverty, is limited to basic skills. Since they use direct instruction anyway, it is not likely they would run into the dilemma being discussed here. Should it come up, however, they would follow the principal's directive to desist, and would inform the children that it is the principal's decision. Again, because they are insensitive to the need for helping to build in poverty children trust for society's institutions, they would not consider the implications of their actions. When asked directly, "Would you tell your children the principal is making you stop?" quitters and failures frequently respond, "I always tell the truth."

This section could have been titled "Response to Authority." It might seem to the uninitiated that it is a situation teachers rarely encounter, and therefore of little importance. That is precisely the point. The less likely the teacher is to be engaged in a project that is objected to in some way by supervisors, principals, other teachers, or janitors, the less likely the teacher is to be engaging students in vital learning activities. There are teachers who complete a 30-year career without ever being faced with this type of dilemma—i.e., the children's learning vs. a school rule. Stars, on the other hand, face this forced choice constantly throughout their careers. Their commitment to children's learning makes it inevitable that someone will be miffed, put out, or downright threatened by the effectiveness of their teaching. If other teachers—and the principal—are failing and under stress, the presence of a successful, happy teacher and class in their midst is extremely threatening. It reminds others of their own inadequacies. Rather than improve and change themselves, the inadequate unite to stamp out effectiveness. This dynamic is among the oldest in U.S. schools. Stars face it daily, and respond with persistence and good humor. Indeed, they are notorious at neutralizing—even befriending—their adversaries.

Generalizations: Putting Ideas into Practice

Some teachers are able to act; they can conceive of numerous specific things to do. They can keep children active and busy. Others are able to conceptualize and verbalize about teaching; they can see purposes and implications, but not necessarily ways to involve children. Stars can do both. They are able to create classroom environments in which children are busy in constructive ways and, at the same time, they can explain the purposes of the activities and their ideological underpinnings. Quitters and failures are unable to do either; they can implement few worthwhile activities with children, and can explain little of why they do what they do. The figure on page 42 shows these four groups.

The importance of connecting ideas with action is that teachers must continually develop and improve themselves. In order for this to happen, they must be able to translate ideas into action. Theories from college courses, principles learned from workshops, and the various ideas they hear or read about must all be translated into practice. In order for such ideas to be useful, teachers must be able to see the action implications of abstract suggestions. This ability to transform theory into practice, i.e., to turn an abstract generalization into a specific set of classroom activities for children, is a vital function performed by stars. Without this ability to move between theory and practice, all forms of teacher education and in-service staff development are wastes of time.

Stars can describe a large number of specific things they do, and combine or synthesize these discrete behaviors into an abstract principle or goal for their instruction. Referring again to the figure below, if we were to begin by giving star teachers an idea or an abstraction in any form, they would be able to come up with a great number of specific behaviors—for themselves and for children. If we were to begin on the action level with only concrete behaviors, stars would be equally

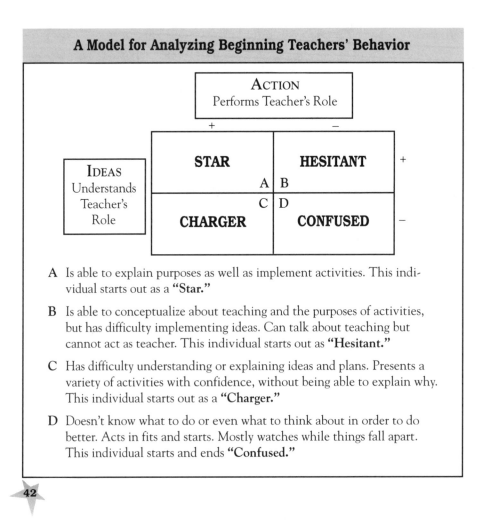

A Model for Analyzing Beginning Teachers' Behavior

	ACTION Performs Teacher's Role	
	+	−
IDEAS Understands Teacher's Role	STAR A	B HESITANT
	C CHARGER	D CONFUSED

A   Is able to explain purposes as well as implement activities. This individual starts out as a **"Star."**

B   Is able to conceptualize about teaching and the purposes of activities, but has difficulty implementing ideas. Can talk about teaching but cannot act as teacher. This individual starts out as **"Hesitant."**

C   Has difficulty understanding or explaining ideas and plans. Presents a variety of activities with confidence, without being able to explain why. This individual starts out as a **"Charger."**

D   Doesn't know what to do or even what to think about in order to do better. Acts in fits and starts. Mostly watches while things fall apart. This individual starts and ends **"Confused."**

competent at explaining and theorizing about the meaning, implications, and values of these behaviors.

This ability of stars to move from action to thought and back to action means that stars continue to grow throughout their careers. They start out ahead, and get better and better. Some teachers have a single year of experience, 30 times. Without the ability to reflect on one's behavior, there is only rote learning. Stars are able to reflect on their experiences, and thereby grow and develop on a career-long basis.

Consider the following generalizations commonly made about teachers: good teachers have high expectations; good teachers believe all children can learn; good teachers use information about the children to teach them more; good teachers involve the children in active learning (Ryans 1960). There seem to be endless generalizations that might be elicited from teachers if they were asked, "What are some things that good teachers believe?" Actually this is not the case. There are many teachers and would-be teachers who cannot respond to this question at all! They are so concrete in their thinking that they can only report specific things that they or other teachers do, but are unable to state any generalization about what these specific behaviors add up to. In effect, they cannot finish the sentence, "A good teacher believes. . . ." A second group refuses to answer the question. Their position is that it is not possible to generalize about people because generalizations are not always true, and making generalizations about people is the same as stereotyping. A third group will not deal with the question because they are convinced that one can only learn by experience, and one person can never speak for another. (This is an especially interesting point of view when heard from elementary teachers who spend most of every day teaching reading. Is the goal of reading to learn by transcending one's life experiences, or to limit oneself to reading only things related to one's own life experiences?) In any event, there are a substantial number of college graduates who simply state that they "can only speak from personal experience" about any issue or topic, and to whom generalizations are useless. In answer to questions such as, "Do you believe World War I really happened?" or "Do you believe a man really landed on the moon?" I have received responses such as, "Now that I think about it, I can't really be certain. I don't necessarily believe everything I read or see on television." This response once again indicates that personal experience is their basis for determining truth. Summarizing the three categories, there are some who can't generalize because they are concrete thinkers, others who won't because they regard it as an evil practice akin to stereotyping, and still others who are totally committed to the idea that personal experience is the only way people

Chapter 3

can claim to know anything.

These are interesting views for individuals who are college graduates and teachers. What we call "knowledge" in the university consists essentially of generalizations grouped into departments,: i.e., generalizations about economics, literature, history, biology, and the other subject areas. These disciplines are all subject to change—new knowledge—and are comprised of concepts that are held to be generally, but not always, true. The standard that generalizations are useless because they are not always true reflects the thinking of an individual who has not really dealt with subjects at a university level, or an individual locked into a level of certainty that is limited to subjects such as ninth-grade geometry, where a right angle is *always* 90 degrees.

Individuals who do not believe it is possible to generalize about teaching— because it is not possible to generalize about anything—make responses such as the following:

Questioner: Do you believe smoking causes lung cancer?
Respondent: Yes.
Questioner: Suppose you found out that less than half of those who smoke die of lung cancer?
Respondent: Well, then, maybe it doesn't. It's an individual matter. A lot of smokers don't die.
Questioner: Do you think drunk drivers cause road fatalities?
Respondent: Yes.
Questioner: Suppose you found out that only about half of the road deaths are caused by drunks?
Respondent: Then it's like I say. It's not always true . . . you can't generalize.

The concept that subject-matter generalizations vary in the *degree* to which they are true is rejected as a way of thinking by such respondents. My own feeling is somewhat different: I believe some college graduates and practicing teachers are not making a value judgment at all. They simply do not have the ability to comprehend gradations of meaning. It is beyond their capacity to understand that phenomena can be valid at varying levels. This issue of the degree to which concepts are true becomes confused in their minds because they can only comprehend the word *true* as absolute. Truth to them is something that must always be true in universal terms—as in religious truth. These people are dangerous to have as teachers of children, since they not only have no understanding of the nature of knowledge but reject this nature. The fact that many of the teachers who are limited in this way are also concrete thinkers does not seem to me to be coincidental. Madison is the one absolute capital of Wisconsin. In base ten, four plus five is always nine. If teachers do not deal in knowledge at all, but confine their teaching to information and basic skills, then this view of the world becomes understandable. Unfortunately for children, they need teachers who can offer them knowledge and thinking, as well as factual information.

There are, of course, other groups of teachers—up through stars—who not only hold many generalizations about good teaching, but who can state the behavioral manifestations of their generalizations (Box A, figure on page 42). For example, consider the following star responses.

Questioner: Please give a generalization you believe about good teaching.

Respondent: Good teachers have high expectations.

Questioner: What might I see you doing in your classroom that would lead me to infer you have high expectations?

Respondent: I wouldn't ignore pupils who were quiet and who might slide by unnoticed.

Questioner: What would you do that we might actually see?

Respondent: I might give them a special assignment, or make sure to include them in a discussion, or maybe simply stand near them.

Questioner: How else is having high expectations demonstrated?

Respondent: Lots of ways. If a child answers an open-ended question with one word, or says "I don't know," or remains quiet, you have to show you believe he or she can do it. I would wait, encourage, take time to listen.

Questioner: Any other ways?

Respondent: Sure. Some children frequently need extra assignments and harder tasks. The children have to see that you are involved emotionally— that you care how well and how much they do. This shows them you believe in their ability and have high goals.

Questioner: How do you demonstrate this caring?

Respondent: By preparing lots of extra things they might do, I demonstrate I care. Also by listening, not overlooking anyone, and not settling for minimums—pushing them to maximums.

Questioner: Again, what does that mean in practice? What do you do to get

Chapter 3

maximums?

Respondent: Basically, you've got to have multiple backup assignments and several things always ready to do. Those children who need more to do should get it; others might need to backtrack and relearn things; others are just less focused and need more help or more options. Whatever level they're on, you've got to keep them actively involved all the time. By emphasizing effort, you can show you believe in them. If you don't stress effort, they'll lapse into believing it's all ability—that you either have it or you don't. That's the last thing you want to have happen to children.

This dialogue stands in sharp contrast to dialogues with failures or quitters, who are (1) frequently unable or unwilling to generalize about what good teachers do, and (2) unable to connect any generalizations with what they mean for the teacher's day-to-day practice. *Without the ability to connect concepts of teaching with specific ways to implement these generalizations, teachers are unable to develop and improve. There can be no "in-service" other than specific suggestions.* On the other hand, teachers with the ability to make this connection, who can tick off ways they can act upon or use an idea, have an unlimited capacity for growth.

The process of connecting ideals—as well as ideas—to behavior is also vital for teachers of children in poverty. The foregoing example (Good teachers have high expectations) is not merely a research-based generalization that can be used to increase student learning. It is also part of star teachers' ideology. The need for teachers of the poor to have both ideas and ideals makes this ability to connect concepts and practice an absolutely required function of teaching.

I have avoided the use of the term *theory* in this discussion because there are no total theories available to teachers. There are unlimited numbers of theoretical propositions, concepts, and principles that have useful implications for teachers, but no overall system for explaining and predicting the teaching and learning that occurs in classrooms. The one exception—behaviorism—is noteworthy since it is completely rejected by stars, well accepted by quitters and failures, and accepted to varying degrees by most teachers in between.

The ability of quitters and failures to connect concepts of teaching with classroom practice is minimal or nonexistent. Given an idea, they cannot suggest a classroom practice that exemplifies it. Given a classroom practice, they cannot explain the concept it illustrates. Consider the following dialogues.

Questioner: Imagine you have observed me teach for half an hour, six days in a row. Each day I tell the whole class to turn to another page in their reading workbook, page 58, 59, 60, etc. The children sit quietly at their desks, all completing the same assignment. Each works quietly in his or her own workbook. What would you infer I believe about good teaching?

Respondent #1: I would think you believed in trusting the children.

Respondent #2: I believe you are organized and have planned well.

Respondent #3: You probably believe in teamwork and will have the children share their answers.

Respondent #4: Would you repeat the question? (This is done several times and the word "infer" is replaced by "think." In many cases, the question is put into first-grade English, e.g., "Guess what I think good teaching is.")

Respondent #5: I would think you were a good teacher.

Respondent #6: I would think you are a bad teacher.

The last two responses initiate a dialogue about not judging the teacher in the example, merely attributing a generalization to him or her. This dialogue usually breaks down. Some respondents are unable to separate description from evaluation.

I realize that many readers will be surprised—shocked—by the inability of certified teachers who are college graduates to deal with even this low level of discourse. I can only report that it happens frequently, and that in the 35 years that I have asked such questions, the responses of quitters and failures have not changed in any substantive way.

This function is not only vital but an absolute necessity to the work of stars. Their ideals are fairly stable over time; however, the pool of ideas they actively seek out to implement their ideals is constantly expanding. They constantly learn more about various subject areas, how children learn together and alone, and the effects on human development of growing up in poverty. As stars pick up new concepts, they can think up numerous ways of implementing them in their classrooms. Just as frequently, stars think in the reverse order. They are attracted by materials, equipment, an activity that will interest their children—and they try it out. But as they endlessly adopt good ideas, they remain completely and sensitively aware of *why* they are doing what they do, *what* they hope to accomplish, and *how* doing it connects with everything else. In contrast to concrete nonthinkers, stars never lose sight of the ideology that undergirds every aspect of life in their classrooms. Even the most seemingly unimportant behaviors of their children and themselves have been thought about and reflected upon in terms of their support for the stars' total view of *why* he or she and the children are there.

Approach to "At-Risk" Children

When identifying language groups and children in poverty, educators substitute terms they consider inoffensive for terms that have become offensive to particular groups (Haberman 1995). These euphemisms inevitably become recognized for what they are—labels and code words. They might appear to be innocuous when they are initially adopted because they are new terms without a clear history. As these new labels are used, however, it soon becomes clear in the public mind and among educators that the same groups are being identified: children with low achievement scores; children who are frequently absent; children whose families move frequently; children who are from poverty backgrounds; children who are most frequently disciplined and suspended; children from dysfunctional families; children with handicapping conditions; children with language problems; children whose parents are not visible in schools; children who are most likely to be victims of crime, physical abuse, and chemical abuse; children who become teenage parents; youth who drop out or who are sent to alternative schools; children and youth of color; or children of non-English-speaking backgrounds. Added to this common list of attributes are all the other children and youth perceived by educators and the public to be "problems" in the schools.

Those with handicapping physical, mental, or social conditions that can be assessed by "experts" are considered to be diagnosed, rather than labeled (Center for the Study of Social Policy 1993). At present, there are approximately 4.5 million children and youth who have been identified as having some form of handicapping condition. By the year 2000, there might well be more than 5 million youngsters in this category. And, if the number of "experts" prepared by schools of education and hired by school districts continues to grow, and the number of urban teachers who perceive children as problems they shouldn't have to deal with continues to increase, this number may reach 20 percent by the year 2020. These figures are staggering when one considers that youngsters diagnosed with some form of handicapping condition are concentrated in the 120 largest U.S. school districts. In other words, these are children who are perceived as *legitimately* labeled because an "expert" has assessed them and testified to an abnormal condition (Hodgkinson 1992).

Approximately 12 million additional children and youth, also concentrated in the largest urban school districts, are labeled "at risk." These are the youngsters who are illegitimately lumped together and labeled on the basis of the several attributes described above. Essentially, they are the children of poverty from diverse cultural backgrounds in our urban school systems (Hodgkinson 1992).

The situation is quite clear. The number of children who are perceived as failing or not doing as well as they should be in school is high. It includes 11 percent labeled because of some handicapping condition, and 25 percent more in poverty. To these numbers should be added those that teachers call "gray-area" children, who seem to fall between the cracks of the system because they are not diagnosed as needing special help, are not necessarily below the poverty line, do not come from minority backgrounds, and yet do not seem to learn much in school. When these groups are added, their numbers exceed 50 percent in almost all urban school districts. This means that urban schools and teachers are defining a majority of their students as children who have problems that exceed the typical classroom teacher's ability to educate them. How is it possible for schools and teachers to define a majority of their clients as people who shouldn't be there, or people they are unable to help?

The answer to this critical question provides the context for understanding the current crisis related to "at-risk" children and youth. In former times U.S. children of the urban masses could skip high school, and still earn a decent living and achieve upward mobility for themselves and their families. Today's schools have accepted the challenge of universal education. And completing high school—even college—no longer assures graduates a better life than their parents (Tyack 1982). The public has come to regard education as a personal rather than a common good, but a scarce resource. Since it is scarce, some—the "top half"—are perceived as having earned the right to enter postsecondary institutions and pursue some sort of career. Others—the "bottom half"—are kept in school because it is a less expensive alternative to welfare or the criminal justice system, and these children should be prepared for the jobs society needs done that are not necessarily careers or a source of upward mobility. In effect, our society accepts and supports an educational system that is ostensibly fair in its competition but that inevitably produces winners and losers. The only issue that seems to remain is how to educate happy, compliant losers rather than antisocial ones. The notion that the people of the United States truly want equal educational opportunity—a scenario in which the children of the poor would actually compete successfully with, and take career opportunities away from, middle-class youngsters who would then perform the menial work of society—is yet to be supported in a credible way.

Against this background—which might be described as the rhetoric of equal opportunity but the reality of an inferior education for children in poverty—we now return to the question: How is it possible for schools and teachers to define a majority of their clients as people who shouldn't be there, or people they are unable to teach? Teachers, and the teacher educators who prepare them, have never been effective with children in poverty. Since 1800, when the children of the London slums were taught in classes of 1,000, with one teacher and a pyramid of monitors, public schools have never provided the urban poor with equal opportunity. The principles and theories we call child and adolescent development were all developed to explain the middle-class experience (Greer 1972). Everyone outside this experience is regarded as an exception, whether immigrant, nonwhite, non-Christian, non-English-speaking, or from a nontraditional family. The entire concept of average or typical—assumed to be universal and taught to future teachers as normal—is, in fact, a parochial middle-class myth. As a result of examining children through a middle-class knothole and defining all others as somehow different or special, the future teacher finishes teacher education not merely unprepared for the real world, but destined to fail in it. Imagine the impact of a teacher education in which middle-class characteristics of child development are taught as universal laws, followed by the assignment of the neophyte to a class in which the majority of children are, by definition, abnormal! Such a fantasy of irrelevant teacher education can only be perpetrated and perpetuated by an education faculty who have themselves never taught in urban schools. And this is precisely the case. Less than one percent of teacher educators have taught in urban schools for three years or more (Haberman 1986a). Teacher educators still raise the question, "What's different about teaching in urban schools?"

As if misleading teacher preparation that teaches "kids are kids," "teaching is teaching," and "learning is learning" is not enough of a handicap, there is also nothing in teacher education programs that counteracts the various forms of prejudice with which all U.S. students begin their teaching careers. Racism, sexism, feelings against non-English-speakers, and, most of all, misconceptions about why people are poor are as common among future teachers as in the population at large. Preservice students' typical explanations of poverty include the full range of stereotypes: the poor are stupid, lazy, without initiative, and lacking moral responsibility for themselves and their families. This combination of a belief in universal principles of child development—which are essentially class attributes—and a range of prejudices and misconceptions about poverty in the United States is the knowledge base with which most certified graduates are launched on a career in urban teaching. On top of these handicaps, the neophyte also begins teaching extremely fearful of discipline—a natural reaction to children and youth one does not understand or respect—and committed to the notion of classroom management as a prerequisite to everything else. The natural consequence of this view of teaching—that the children are all problems or potential problems—is a childlike acceptance of direct instruction and behavior modification. As detailed earlier, this merely makes a bad situation worse, and predestines the beginners prepared in traditional university programs to quit or fail.

To return to the basic issue, dysfunctional teacher education is a major part of the explanation for why a *majority* of children and youth are defined as exceptional or special in most urban school districts. The essential point is that to define them otherwise would imply that there was something wrong with the teachers themselves, with the faculty who prepare the teachers, or with the school curricula offered to these problem children. In other words, the forced choice perceived by teachers is between defining themselves as inadequate or the children as lacking in some form of essential development or knowledge.

Blaming the victim is an active pastime of schools and educators. It is an occupational disease. In former times we used terms such as culturally deprived, socially deprived, culturally disadvantaged, academically disadvantaged, underdeveloped, disaffected, difficult to serve, hard to reach, alienated, and a host of others. All of these terms, including the present "at risk," are labels used for the same purpose: to attribute the causes of low achievement and school failure to the child and family, but to do so in a manner that implies the labeler is not prejudiced and is sincerely trying to help. There is no way to provide a hopeful or an equal education to a child that one perceives and labels as basically inadequate.

The reason the process of labeling children in poverty never ceases is that there are only two alternatives: either there is something wrong with the child and his or her background, or there is something wrong with the teacher's methods and school curricula. Either the child must change, or the school must. If there is success, it is likely that teachers and schools will assume the credit, as in most upper-class suburbs and private schools. If there is widespread failure, as in urban schools, then blame and responsibility is more readily placed on the victims. To do otherwise would mean that schools and teachers do not know enough, or do not do things as well as they should.

Star teachers differ from failures and quitters by how they approach this question. If asked to explain the large number of children and youth at risk of failing or dropping out, most teachers go through the same litany of causes that most other U.S. citizens do: dysfunctional families, drugs, violence, gangs, lack of nutrition, poor housing, unemployment, crime, lack of belief in education, no role models, and inherent defects. The quitters and failures never mention schools and teachers. If specifically asked, "How do you explain the large numbers of children behind in basic skills?" they still make no attribution whatever to schools, curricula, teachers, or teaching methods. They see only the victim and his or her own faults. On the basis of this perception, when quitters or failures are asked to propose solutions to the problems of at-risk students, they make no reference to schools at all. They propose ways in which all the other agencies of society, outside of schools, might help families and children improve their lives and perhaps prepare children and parents to benefit from school. Not only do they not see schools and curricula needing to become more responsive, they do not consider that they as teachers must change what they do. Indeed, they justify their perceptions with comments such as, "You can't be all things for all people," or "You can't expect schools and teachers to do everything for people," or "With 30 in a class, trying to teach reading, what am I supposed to do about hunger or child abuse?" There is a great similarity between the views of quitters and failures and the responses of U.S. citizens in general to these questions of who and what must be changed.

Star teachers know all the same explanations of what's wrong with the families and communities in which their children live. However, when asked about the causes of at-risk children and youth, stars answer entirely differently. They first recognize the impact of the label "at risk" on all who use it. They then emphasize a wide variety of ways in which school curricula and teaching methods cause large numbers of children to be at risk. They make the locus of their explanation the school. They describe how irrelevant curriculum and authoritarian and boring instruction exacerbate the problems that children bring to school. Essentially, stars say, "Look, I have the most control over what and how I teach. I should be able to find a way to involve my children in learning, no matter what their out-of-school lives are like. That's my job, and that's what I work at until I find activities and projects that work—that turn them on to learning." This is not to imply that stars are insensitive to the problems and impact of poverty. They merely focus on their role as teachers.

How one approaches at-risk students is a critical point for discriminating among teachers and would-be teachers and for predicting success in teaching children in poverty. Quitters and failures justify their lack of effectiveness by detailing inadequacies in the children. They frequently seem to want to know as much as possible about their children for the purpose of proving to themselves that teaching these children is impossible. Stars, on the other hand, learn about their children's lives for entirely different motives. They seek to become sensitive to the children's backgrounds because they genuinely care about them. In some cases they seek information because they can help with a referral to an agency, or to report some sort of abuse that must be addressed. Most typically, stars want to learn about children's out-of-school lives because they want to make learning more meaningful and relevant. Information about their students enables stars to make specific connections between a learning activity in class and something that will clinch its meaning for the individual child. Stars also know that by listening to what their children choose to tell them about their lives, they are deepening the bonds of mutual respect between themselves and the children. In sum, quitters and failures do not necessarily know less about their children than stars. The critical distinction is whether they use this information to "prove" the children cannot be taught or to make their teaching more relevant.

Of all the functions that discriminate between stars and failures, this dimension is the most powerful predictor. There is no question that those predisposed to blame the victim will fail as teachers, while those whose natural inclination is constantly to seek more effective teaching strategies, regardless of youngsters' backgrounds or the obstacles youngsters face, have a fighting chance of becoming effective teachers of children in poverty.

Many teachers have so completely internalized the process of blaming the victim and not holding schools or themselves even partly responsible for children's failure that they are not even aware they are doing so. By not specifically stating that a particular race or ethnic group has lower native intelligence, many teachers believe they have avoided blaming the children. They simply do not comprehend that by blaming the economy, the parents, or the peers for the fact that a majority of poverty children are failing in basic skills, they are still centering the locus of fault in the children's inadequacies. What it means when the only reason teachers give for a child being at risk is that a child's home life is inadequate or that parents don't care is that they are shifting responsibility away from themselves. Until there are more effective strategies for selecting and training teachers for children in poverty, quitters, failures, and many other educators will continue the traditional way of explaining student failure: the problems are with the children—not necessarily their fault, but in the children, nonetheless. To locate the problem elsewhere would not only cast aspersions on present forms of schooling, teaching, and teacher education, but would imply that all those involved should be more competent, or at least trying to do more.

Professional-Personal Orientation to Students

Do star teachers believe they must love their children in order to teach them? Do stars believe the children must love them in order to be able to learn in their classrooms? The answer to both questions is "no." Stars use words like caring, respect, and trust. In many cases stars do, of course, love their children, but they do not regard love as a prerequisite condition for teaching a child, or as a method of teaching. They know that love is not enough. One must also know what to teach and how to teach. Stars are keenly aware of and honest about the fact that many of the children they teach are not lovable and do not necessarily engage in lovable behaviors—toward others, themselves, or those who would be their teachers.

As with all the other functions of star teachers, this one is a combination of teacher behaviors and the ideology that undergirds their behaviors. The orientation of the teacher to the child around this love issue goes to the very heart of questions such as: Why does an individual seek to become a teacher? Why does an individual remain in teaching? How does a teacher attempt to relate to his or her students? How does a teacher manage a classroom, and practice discipline? What personal needs—outside of occupational and monetary—is a teacher seeking to satisfy by teaching children in poverty?

The orientation of star teachers reflects an ideology that answers each of these questions in terms of what's best for the children, and not in terms of satisfying the teacher's needs or preferences. Stars establish very close and supportive relationships with most of the children they teach. These relationships have many aspects of a love relationship. But stars recognize the dangers of such relationships, and do not fall into the trap of needing children's love for their own emotional support. They understand that the basic goal of the teacher is to connect children with meaningful learning in ways that are interesting to the learners. To have the children obey, comply, follow directions, and engage in meaningless lessons because the teacher will love them in return is the basic strategy of failures and quitters, not stars. When failures realize that not even the "nice" children will do everything they direct them to do because they love them, and that there are many children they cannot love at all, they frequently panic. They realize their pet cliche, i.e., "I want to be a teacher because I love all children," is not a strategy for either teaching or controlling children in their class-rooms.

Many parents control their children by promoting guilt. They use hurt feelings and disappointment to control their children's behavior. "If you really love me, you will do this and not that." Or, "If you really love me, you will do this even if you find it upsetting or difficult. Do it for me!" This ability to generate guilt by using love appears to "work" for many parents, if by "work" we mean they can control some of their children's behaviors. Actually, it more frequently does not "work" because children do not develop an intrinsic desire to engage in the behaviors parents prefer, and once they are not directly supervised they will frequently do the opposite of what their parents sought. Psychologists and psychiatrists do a thriving business with adults unable to define or pursue any intrinsically developed life goals because they were guilt-ridden by parents who used love in this manner (Bettelheim 1965).

Teachers, of course, are not in the role of parents. It is quite easy for many, particularly teachers of younger or needier children, to assume the parental role. This appears to be a workable relationship for many teachers as they relate to many children. There are, however, critical differences between stars and failures in this regard. Stars do not use children to meet some personal need or lack in their own lives. They have spouses, families, friends, and others in their lives who meet their emotional needs outside of school. They are not wounded healers seeking to compensate for what is missing in their lives by feeding emotionally on children. They care deeply about and thoroughly respect their children—caring particularly about their children's learning and love of learning—but there is also some life space that separates them from the children in their classrooms. Stars also show their caring and respect for the children by not exploiting their warm and close relationship. The trust that stars build with children enables them to serve as successful models. Children see star teachers as people they care about, who care about them, and who engage in particular behaviors of learning; and the children seek—voluntarily—to try out some of those behaviors as well, e.g., reading for enjoyment, writing to express oneself, conducting experiments, building models, speaking other languages, using computers, applying math, asking and answering endless questions, etc. In this way stars who build trusting, warm, loving, respectful relationships with children serve as models. After stars engage, interest, and hook their children, the children develop intrinsic reasons for pursuing learning activities.

Star teachers are sensitive and aware. They are entirely conscious of how they may have used their close relationship with children to initially model an activity. Perhaps, in this first instance, there was some extrinsic reward. The children may have tried out a subject or activity to please the teacher. Perhaps, in the beginning, stars are successful models by exploiting their trust relationship with the children to get them involved initially—to try out particular learning activities. The modeling effect frequently affects children in this way: "If Ms. Smith enjoys it so much—and cares so much that I give it a try—maybe I will." But stars are sensitive to this dynamic and work hard to quickly shift the impetus for children's work to the children's choices, *their* plans, *their* follow-through, and the satisfactions *they* derive from pursuing an activity in depth. In short, stars may start out using modeling as a viable teaching strategy, but they recognize the need to shift the reason for children's persistence in learning activities from the rewards of a caring adult to the intrinsic joys that children experience and derive from becoming self-directed learners.

Stars are also sensitive to the reality that there will be children, perhaps several in each class, who are not prime candidates for "lovable child of the year." Their approach to these children is equally caring and respectful of their potential. Stars realize that if they made "love" the prerequisite to their teaching, they would have to write off some children in every class. Stars are sensitive to the reality that, as teachers, they must be aware of their children's life conditions and must become directly involved by making referrals and seeking the help of resource people when they identify cases of abuse, neglect, and health emergencies. At the same time, stars are very careful about intruding on their children's life space. They do not seek personal information for its own sake, nor do they offer unsolicited advice regarding matters that are not directly related to learning in the classroom.

Thus far, I have discussed specific star behaviors related to how they model learning behavior and perhaps use their relation-

ship with children to initially attract them to an activity, shifting to strategies that foster children's intrinsic motivation such as having children participate in planning, carrying out, and evaluating their studies. Stars are also concerned about the love issue as it relates to classroom management and discipline. They set up rules for classroom, school, and field-trip behavior that are few in number but have logical consequences for themselves and the children. The reasons for the guidelines are discussed with children so that everyone sees their sense and usefulness from the outset. Stars never seek to manipulate a child with guilt ("How could you do this to me after I trusted you?"). Stars expect and plan for the times when even their most lovable children will engage in negative behaviors. Stars' reaction is not to demonstrate disappointment and a sense of being betrayed, but to patiently pursue the logical consequences of whatever has occurred. The stars' ability and strength to support and nurture children who have engaged in wrongful acts derives from the fact that they truly do care about their children and have not fallen into the trap of having an unreflective love relationship with them. In sum, stars have a relationship with children that demonstrates a consciously premeditated caring. Such caring is not predicated on children always doing the right thing. On the contrary, it assumes they frequently will not. At that point the professional caring springs into action and demonstrates to the child that he or she is worthy and capable—even at the lowest and worst moment of his or her offense. Stars show children not that "you have hurt me and let me down," but that some things have occurred that are unwise or regrettable but "we're in this together and can work it out." In effect, "I'm here for you."

What this adds up to is that stars have infinitely greater emotional stamina than most other teachers. They may have invested countless hours in and after school with individual youngsters, only to see him or her move on to dropping out, drugs, teenage pregnancy, and even death. Nevertheless, they continue to invest themselves in their children. I recently spoke with two middle school star teachers who had children in their classrooms murdered in the same week. They were consumed with grief and could not discuss the children without weeping. However, they still continued to invest great time and energy in making individual commitments to their children's learning. By not using such instances of personal tragedy to distance themselves from their children, stars demonstrate great emotional stamina. They are "strong-sensitives" who are capable of knowing and understanding the life problems of their students for the purpose of making school learning more alive and more relevant. Stars care deeply, but they keep going because there are other children to be taught who need their services.

This approach to demonstrating respect and caring rather than some form of intimate love for students distinguishes stars from other teachers in several basic functions of teaching. Stars use their personal relationships to model learning and enhance the teaching-learning process. A second basic function that is performed differently by stars and quitters is the use of personal relationships to discipline and manage children. Quitters and failures frequently adopt "love" as a teaching strategy because they try to use guilt in much the same way as some parents do. They assume that, by loving and being loved in return, they can control. After all, "you wouldn't do anything nasty to someone who loves you." When quitters and failures soon learn that children "they have done everything for" still misbehave or, even worse, do not feel guilty for doing so, they have lost the basic teaching strategy they depended on for classroom management. I refer to this form of teacher manipulation as the "iron hand in the velvet glove." It is especially common among kindergarten and primary teachers who are superficially "nice" but who teach by giving directions and providing the extrinsic reward of their "love" to those who obey, i.e., "cooperate." For these reasons quitters and failures are chary about accepting positions in urban schools; they know they cannot bring themselves to love all the children and youth they will encounter. They are also fairly sure that all the children will not necessarily love them. Without such love they know they will not be able to use guilt as a teaching strategy.

There are individuals who take the position that the teacher must love and be loved in order to teach. Consider the following dialogue.

Questioner: Is it necessary for you to love all the children in order to be able to teach them?

Respondent: Yes. I love all children.

Questioner: You've never met a child you didn't love?

Respondent: Not yet.

Questioner: Can you imagine a child in your class that's not necessarily lovable?

Respondent: I can, but I separate the child from his behavior. I may not like what he does, but I will love him.

Questioner: You will love a child who slashes your tires?

Respondent: As I said, I separate the behavior from the person. I may not like what a child does, but I will love each one of them. Love is the basis on which teaching is built.

Questioner: Can you imagine a child who might not love you?

Respondent: Yes.

Questioner: Will you be able to teach such a child?

Respondent: Yes.

Questioner: Why is it necessary for you to love each child but for that child to not necessarily love you?

Respondent: Over time that child will come to appreciate what I'm trying to do for him.

Questioner: I'm not asking about "appreciation." Are you saying the child must love you to learn from you?

Respondent: It surely helps and will make my job easier.

Questioner: I want to be certain I understand. You believe that love—not caring, respect, liking—but your love for the student is a prerequisite for you to teach him or her.

Respondent: It's the best basis for teaching.

Questioner: Do you love everyone now in the Cook County Jail?

Respondent: (Pause) I'm not sure. Probably not.

Questioner: Is it possible that you might be able to teach something to some of the

Chapter 3

inmates?

Respondent: (Pause) Perhaps, I'm not sure.

Questioner: In any event, we can be clear. Your view is that love is the best basis for children to learn and for teachers to teach.

Respondent: Right.

This interview is predictive of failure. Mutual love is regarded as the basis for teaching and learning. These expectations are shattered in urban classrooms when teachers find that they can only pretend to love every child, and that many of the children feel no obligation to pretend. I recall a beginning teacher in a middle school classroom sitting at her desk quietly weeping while the class was in chaos. This teacher confided to me, "I don't know why they behave this way. I love them. I take them places every weekend. I bring them to my home in the evenings. I really love these kids." At the end of the period as the children filed out, a student put her arm around the still-weeping teacher and said encouragingly, "Don't take it personal, Mrs. Barnes; that's the way kids are."

Perceptions related to the loving of children are frequently extrapolations of the maternal care young children need. Demonstrations of affection are not a method of teaching. Would we be as sanguine with this approach if our vision was a 25-year-old teacher hugging a 17-year-old student for answering correctly? I doubt it.

The function described here reflects stars' ideology for relating to students so students learn more and develop a love of learning. Stars relate closely to children and youth but do not intrude on their life space and do not use their relationship to resolve any of their own unmet emotional needs. Stars seek to create learners who will be independent and not need them; quitters and failures seek the reverse—students who will be entirely dependent on the teacher's approval. Stars do not see love as a strategy for managing classroom discipline. Failures do. Finally, while stars exploit their close, positive relations with students to model the joys of learning, they seek ways to move children on to gain intrinsic value from learning.

The Care and Feeding of the Bureaucracy

Star teachers are extremely sensitive to the fact that they work in mindless bureaucracies. They know quite well that, in large urban school systems, teachers are treated as bureaucratic functionaries, and not professionals. If they are ill and out a day, the only adult likely to be aware of it is the school secretary responsible for calling substitute teachers. Now there are computer call-ups for substitute teachers,

60

so that even the school secretary doesn't know who's sick. There are some excellent individual schools in every urban district, but not one school system that can be described as excellent—or even satisfactory. To the uninitiated, the school bureaucracy is regarded as an organized set of administrators and procedures that simply impede the process of schooling. To able, experienced teachers in urban school systems, however, the school bureaucracy is recognized as a structure that has been systematically organized to prevent effective teaching and learning. It is not uncommon for a typical classroom to be interrupted over 100 times per week, if the intercom, visitors, emergencies, office requests, other teachers, various messengers, and students coming and going are all counted. I consulted in a high school that was part of a prison for juvenile offenders. Everyone, from the superintendent to the janitor, agreed that nothing was more important for these youngsters than their education. The rhetoric of this institution placed learning ahead of any other priority, yet in one week we counted 125 interruptions in the average classroom. If a barber showed up, the students were excused from class to get a haircut. Those unused to the ways of bureaucracy might think that youngsters who are "there," i.e., prisoners, all day and all night, including weekends, could get haircuts at other times. Those who know school bureaucracies are well aware of the realities; if a particular time is more convenient for the barber and for the school administrators who employ him, then that will take precedence. I cite this as merely one example. If in a completely controlled situation—a prison—in which everyone agrees that learning is the top priority, there are still 125 interruptions per week, imagine what occurs in a less controlled school bureaucracy! Experienced urban teachers have become so inured to these interruptions that they have learned to cope with endless intrusions on their work. Only a few still think about cutting the wires on their intercom.

The 120 largest urban school systems have become self-serving bureaucracies organized for the convenience and the maintenance of everyone who works in them—except classroom teachers and students. Typically, there is a 1 to 1 ratio between classroom teachers and other certificated personnel hired to help them (Chubb and Moe 1990). This means that, without counting bus drivers or cafeteria workers—just counting paraprofessionals, aides, assistant principals, principals, guidance counselors, school psychologists, social workers, community liaison people, nurses, special reading teachers, resource teachers, Chapter 1 teachers, specialists, and the cast of thousands in the central offices—there is one licensed professional *without* a class load for each classroom teacher with a regular classroom or full class load. In simple terms, this means that classes in urban schools could be cut in half if all certificated personnel actually taught. If only half of these "teacher helpers" actually taught, then class size could be cut by 33 percent, which means there would be 8 to 10 fewer children in a typical urban classroom.

This situation of a top-heavy bureaucracy is sufficiently devastating when considering the ratio usually cited. In truth, this ratio is 3 to 2 in many urban school systems. In the system with which I am most familiar, there are approximately 6,400 professionals "helping" 4,200 classroom teachers.

This phenomenon of rampant urban school bureaucracy is a reflection of big-city political activity that is as American as apple pie. The primary goal is for the bureaucracy to feed itself and grow—always at the expense of the children it ostensibly serves. Politicians and others in depressed urban areas actually take credit for providing jobs for many in these bloated bureaucracies. A typical ploy of urban schools is to count almost all certificated staff as "instructional" and then to divide the total number of children in the school district by this total number of "instructional" staff. For this reason, on paper, many of our urban school districts show class sizes of 19 or 20 while actual class sizes are as high as 35 or more. This ploy is an old one but still quite effective with education reporters who typically believe and report the class-size data supplied by system administrators.

The generalizations I am making here apply to countless smaller urban school districts as well as to the 120 largest ones. I have worked with a small urban district in Indiana that has fewer than 480 teachers who have full workloads teaching children. This small staff of teachers is "helped" by a $3.5 million budget for administrative staff and other school personnel. Five of the seven city council persons are employees of the school district. There are four athletic directors. An individual is hired to make the daily announcements in the high school at an annual salary of approximately $30,000. Yet, the school district is legally defined as bankrupt. Most children have outdated or no texts. In some classes the teacher uses the only textbook. Text manufacturers won't sell the district new ones because of unpaid bills dating back 12 years.

These unconscionable bureaucracies frequently consume superintendents, who come and go. They also make certain that any state laws or school board policies are transformed or circumvented so that the bureaucracy will continue to survive and grow. The characteristics of these bureaucracies are as follows:

1. They are highly centralized. This overcentralization has many levels in a chain of command.

2. The orientation of the chain of command is downward. Ideas and policies originate with and come from higher levels. Lower levels are to comply and implement. Intelligence and power are assumed to be higher as one moves up the chain of command.

3. This downward orientation of directives generates an upward flow of misinformation and disinformation from anxious subordinates, who desperately seek to justify their past performance and continued existence. The information and data generated upward is inevitably incorrect, or consists of outright lies. For example, no major urban school system in the United States knows precisely how many people it employs, the number of its dropouts, how much particular programs cost, or countless other basic data needed to operate efficiently and honestly. This lack of administrative control reflects more than self-serving bureaucrats. Urban school districts offer an extremely large number of programs, and confuse matters further by commingling federal, state, local and private sources of funds.

4. The organizational structure leads to an inevitable isolation of units that are supposed to be working together. The rewards of the bureaucracy—jobs, salary increases, security—are derived from units not working together and thus risking greater accountability.

5. Particular administrative units seek to expand themselves. There is an inevitable and constant war among organizational units, all of which are irrelevant to teachers and children, to compete for and win higher budgets. Team pride or chauvinism develops among these bureaucratic units.

6. There is irresistible pressure from peers, superiors, and subordinates to support the bureaucracy—and their unit in the bureaucracy—at the expense of meeting the stated goal of the system—more learning for students. Whistleblowers are not common and must be protected by law.

7. Compulsive rule-following and the enforcement of rules is typically used to derail any serious change effort, no matter how well financed or widely supported that change effort might be.

8. Central office and other "facilitators" become more divorced from teachers and children every day. After a short time, they have little or no direct contact or feedback. Isolation from reality inevitably becomes almost total.

9. Decisions are typically made by committee. Careful notes are kept. Individuals are neither held responsible nor are they personally accountable, e.g., "It was decided that . . ."

10. Lower-level and middle-level bureaucrats, while playing a cloying and subservient role to higher levels (superintendents, school board members, etc.), know that they must survive beyond them. Superintendents come and go. They sabotage the top-down directives by overconformity—applying all the rules will kill anything—or by rebelling against those directives that they perceive will ultimately fail. Bureaucrats don't want to go down with a superintendent or superior. They frequently use teachers, parents, or students as the excuse for not implementing a directive.

These characteristics and others are common practices in urban school bureaucracies. They help to explain why middle- and lower-level bureaucrats tend to remain, while top ones change. Even worse, they provide insight into the sickness of bureaucratic structures that are organized to perpetuate and enlarge themselves at the expense of the teachers, children, and parents.

The difficulty is that this analysis leads to various forms of inaction that are as detrimental as the dysfunctional bureaucracies themselves. Critics of public education, and those who are opposed to helping children in poverty gain equal educational opportunity, use this explanation of the bureaucracy to justify cutting school budgets or keeping them minimal: "You can't throw money at these problems!" or "These people are just poor managers selling out their own people!" At the other end of the political spectrum are those who advocate that adults in urban areas need jobs to provide stability to decaying communities, and the fact that the school system provides a number of jobs at least "puts money into the community." Both extremes are, of course, misguided, and merely serve to protect the failing bureaucracy from change.

For more than 30 years, private foundations, state legislatures, the business community, and local citizens' groups have attempted to fight the school bureaucracy by supporting community control, parent control, decentralizations, site-based management, neighborhood school boards, schools of choice, and charter schools. In spite of truly heroic efforts, the urban school bureaucracies not only remain but continue to expand, while class size and teacher load continue to grow. It is now common for many elementary and middle school classrooms in urban areas to have more than 30 children in a class!

Star teachers are aware of all these trends. While they are sensitive to and conscious of how they and their children are being exploited by their system bureaucracies, they spend little or no effort tilting against these windmills. They adjust and cope in ways that enable them to succeed because they are aware of the inevitable pressures coming from the bureaucracy. Quitters and failures, on the other hand, are typically crushed by their school bureaucracies because they are insensitive to their pressures and, therefore, take no actions to mitigate their negative influences. Burnout is the occupational disease faced by all urban teachers. The following analysis details the differences in ideology and behaviors between stars and others as they seek to prevent or resolve the organizational pressures on teachers, almost all of which are negative. These are pressures to do less, try less, work in isolation, blame the victim, and assume that all the people who work in urban schools—where there are more "facilitators" than teachers—have the welfare of children and not their own jobs and convenience as their overriding goal.

Stars recognize that even good teachers burn out, that the organizational press of a defective bureaucracy is an inevitable source of constant stress. They protect themselves in several ways: by learning which rules and policies must be obeyed and which can be ignored; by learning which clerical demands must be done, which can be delayed, and which can be put off indefinitely; and by learning how to throw out most of what is in their mailboxes and deal with the fewest items possible (beginning teachers and failures can easily spend an hour a day reading useless nonsense). This quality—the care and feeding of the bureaucracy—is a critical part of stars' craft. They don't want to threaten or anger the bureaucrats. At the same time, they want to spend as little time as possible on clerical tasks, directives, record keeping, and the endless chores of maintaining the bureaucracy that do not help them teach children and that drain their precious time and energy. As a result, stars become expert at how their bureaucracy works, not because they try to change it but because they seek to do the absolute least that is necessary to feed it and, in return, be left alone. I recall one star teacher with several large cartons of papers in her closet. I asked what they were and she slyly winked and replied that they were notices from the school office and system offices. She said she had saved the last three years' worth and was planning to read them when she retired four years hence.

This function of protecting themselves from an injurious bureaucracy is a critical set of behaviors for stars. A comfort level is reached and maintained fairly early in their careers. As they gain in experience, they hone their skills of knowing what to read and what to discard, which meetings to attend and which to skip, which efforts to volunteer for and which will be a fool's errand, which duties to perform and which to have a child or parent aide perform, when to fill out forms and when to telephone, when to have a discussion and when to ignore an issue. With these skills, stars are able to devote almost all their time and energy to their children and to teaching. Without these skills and lacking the sensitivity that they even need

Chapter 3

such skills, failures and quitters are worn down by the system and can only teach with a portion of their available time and energy. This function is strange in the sense that, if it is done well, few will recognize the need for it or its importance. If ignored or not well done, the unwieldy bureaucracy becomes a formidable obstacle to the work of the teacher. I have read and analyzed countless lists of what teachers supposedly need in order to be effective, and have never seen any expert on instruction point to the need for this critical function. Yet, it is vital to the success of star teachers. I have never interviewed one who has not recognized the function and been willing to explain in detail how to perform it.

In addition to protecting themselves, stars have an even more important stake in the care and feeding of the bureaucracy. They seek to protect their children. They place themselves between their children and the gears of the mindless system. In addition to interruptions, schools have endless rules about not taking more than a certain number of field trips per week or month, insurance coverage, who is and who is not allowed to enter the classroom and under what conditions, the kinds of materials and equipment that can be brought into classrooms, the nature of animals and plants that may be kept, what and who is responsible on weekends for material and living things, and on and on. Technically, a teacher cannot have his or her class walk around the block without a series of permissions. For example, what constitutes decorating a room vs. interfering with unionized painters or breaking the fire code?

Star teachers learn as much as possible about the informal structure of the school as quickly and as well as possible, in order to avoid falling victim to the formal organization of the school. They know which janitor, which secretary, which safety guard, which other teachers will help them do what they want with the least paperwork, permissions, or hassle. Stars are experts at using this informal structure to make the system work for their children. Where quitters and failures are constantly frustrated by running into brick walls, the children in stars' classrooms are engaged in real learning activities—many of which are against school policy or, more likely, unknown to the formal bureaucracy.

A major function of stars' teaching behavior is to make learning as real and as relevant as possible for their children. This requires that their classrooms have more materials and equipment than others. It also means they may have things not normally seen in schoolrooms, from living things to greasy parts of a lawn mower. Stars also implement this reality by taking more field trips than others. They also spill over into other rooms, laboratories, and spaces throughout the school. This function—using materials, space, and direct experience to make learning real—

inevitably brings stars into conflict with the school bureaucracy. When stars add the function of protecting their classes from interruptions, schedule changes, and clerical and other bureaucratic demands, it soon becomes apparent that, in one way or another, they are in an almost constant posture of mitigating the impact of the school bureaucracy. Without the ability to perform this function—developed to a high level of skill—stars would not be

able to teach. Nowhere is the irrelevancy and failure of traditional forms of teacher education as clear and as obvious as in its inability to prepare teachers to perform this function. Young adults are certified and sent to their demise by school of education faculty ignorant of or unable to deal with urban school bureaucracies. Fifty percent of new teachers quit in five years. In many districts, 50 percent are gone in three years (Haberman 1989a)!

A final note is in order. Stars do not function as complete isolates. In ideal situations, they set up networks of colleagues who are like-minded and who serve as a support group. In more typical situations, they set up a support group of individuals who may not all be teachers because there are not sufficient numbers of teachers who use their methods. In many cases stars use several support groups: certain individuals may agree with one aspect of their teaching, e.g., their use of field trips, while others may support their use of computers. They know which associates and colleagues they can depend on for what. It is not unusual for star teachers to have a support network of teachers from various schools so that there is a sufficient number in the group. Such support networks counteract burnout by offering teachers mutual support and by generating activities that provide sustenance to the group members. This is a more powerful antidote for burnout than individual teachers left to their own devices who can only talk over problems with a spouse or a priest, or who must look to a college course for renewal.

There are other mindless bureaucracies besides schools. U.S. society is replete with governmental organizations and private companies whose structures work against them rather than for them. Successful people in all walks of life deal with the function described here. It is unfortunate for the children and youth in our large urban districts that only star teachers and a very few others are capable of performing this function. Perhaps the naive idealism that schools shouldn't be this way prevents teachers—and those who prepare them—from learning to perform this extremely vital set of functions.

Fallibility

When teachers are asked, "Do you ever make mistakes?" they answer, "Of course, I'm only human!" or "Everyone makes mistakes." The difference between stars and quitters is in the nature of the mistakes they recognize and own up to. Quitters and failures talk about misspelling a word or getting an answer wrong in an arithmetic problem. They might admit to transcribing a wrong grade onto a report card. Essentially, they are admitting to slips, typos, and inadvertent, minor errors. Stars, on the other hand, confess to serious errors: misjudging a child, writing off a child by underestimating his or her ability, and, most frequently, blaming and publicly embarrassing the wrong child for something. This occurs because excellent teachers know their children quite well. They are conversant with children's records regarding behavior such as fighting. Their confessed errors relate to reaching judgment too quickly about which child may have initiated a problem situation, without getting all the facts. Such misjudgments occur very rarely with stars, but they are willing to admit that these instances might occur. Quitters and failures simply cannot own up to anything that is serious, or involves human relationships.

Another major difference between the two groups is what they do about mistakes. How do they correct them? For quitters who talk merely about minor slips, corrections are no trouble at all. For stars who are willing to confess to serious misjudgments that endanger the rapport and trust they have established with children, correcting mistakes is messy and takes some doing. Stars are aware, for example, that if they criticize, blame, or accuse a child publicly, they must apologize and rectify the situation publicly. They do not criticize in public and apologize in private. When quitters or failures are presented with hypothetical situations in which they might have blamed the wrong child, they find it difficult, if not impossible, to apologize. Consider the following dialogue:

Questioner: Imagine that Franklin has been taking things from his neighbor's desk all year. When something important is missing, you blame Franklin in front of the class. Later on, another child confesses to the misdeed. What would you do?

Teacher #1: I'd take Franklin aside and explain to him that I misjudged him because he's always taking things. I'd want him to understand that, if he didn't misbehave, I wouldn't have accused him.

Questioner: You'd talk to him privately.

Teacher #1: Yes.

Questioner: Would you apologize?

Teacher #1: I might or might not use the word, but I'd indicate I was sorry. Franklin has to understand that his behavior all year is also part of the reason I accused him.

This reluctance to admit to serious errors is typical of teachers who have a problem owning mistakes. In some cases they appear to be fearful of admitting them, as if something will happen to their stature in the eyes of the children. In other cases they seem to be unable to admit making mistakes because they believe competent, intelligent people don't really make any. Whatever the cause of their reluctance, they rarely suggest that they would correct any serious mistakes publicly. As in the dialogue above, they do not see the need to correct public mistakes in public, and, when they do speak to a child they may have misjudged, they are as likely to emphasize past misdeeds as a way of explaining away their mistake as they are to apologize. In interviews with prospective teachers, it is not uncommon to find candidates who will not or cannot proffer any mistakes at all! After agreeing that everyone makes mistakes and that it is only human to do so, such candidates will sit quietly for 30 seconds or more and then state, "I know I'll make some; I just can't think of what they might be right now."

This dimension is very critical. It is highly predictive of teachers' future classroom behavior. Individuals who cannot admit, recognize, or abide mistakes in themselves are not likely to be tolerant of others' mistakes. An individual who believes he or she has somehow done something wrong, or is a lesser person for having made a mistake, is likely to feel this way about others. Teaching is the worst possible job for such a person! Children not only make mistakes all day, every day,

Chapter 3

but many of their errors are serious ones involving human relations and matters of friendship and trust. It is in the nature of life in the classroom for mistakes to be a recurrent and typical condition.

Stars, who in practice make many fewer serious mistakes, are quite open and revealing about them. Indeed, they frequently find this question humorous, and enjoy revealing various mistakes. As in all the previous functions, fallibility is a combination of stars' ideology and their practice. Because they hold a set of beliefs about the naturalness of fallibility, they are led to behave in human and humane ways when mistakes occur. On a behavioral level, teacher and pupil mistakes are often treated as causes for humor, and the mistakes celebrated as an example of how adults as well as children all need to do better. Stars frequently model this acceptance of mistakes, and on occasion use it as a teachable moment. Consider the following example.

A star second-grade teacher was making certain that all the children in his class knew their addresses and phone numbers, including the ability to write them correctly. On checking, one of the brightest girls in the class whispered to him privately, "I can't write the name of the street I live on." In a loud voice the teacher made this child's confession public, and teased her. "Sandra, who is so bright and so hard-working, can't write her address. I'm really surprised. This is terrible. Now, Sandra, tell me where you live; I'll write it on the blackboard and you copy it down. Then you can learn it. Now, where do you live?" If the teacher would have checked the class register, he would have seen that Sandra's street had a long Native American name (Aneskumonnica). Instead, he embarrassed Sandra first and then waited, poised at the blackboard, to show her the correct spelling. When Sandra told the teacher her street name, he couldn't spell it and was embarrassed. He immediately apologized profusely in front of the class and then enlisted the help of the class. This turned out to be a project because the street was only one block long, and the street sign had been taken. Some children checked with neighbors; others checked with the post office. Three different spellings turned up for the street on different records and documents. The teacher kept referring to his mistake every time a child produced another spelling. For the rest of the year, the teacher found appropriate occasions to remind children of his mistake and model more reasonable behavior. For example, if a child answered too quickly, or didn't check his or her work, or laughed at another child's answer, the teacher would say, "Is that really true, or are we repeating my mistake? Is this another Aneskumonnica?" And everyone would laugh and check what they were doing.

The importance of fallibility cannot be overstated. Beginning in third grade, and especially for males, classroom climates can become extremely competitive in poverty schools. It is common to see children working at the blackboard being derided by catcalls and epithets from fellow students. The climate established in such classrooms is that mistakes are not supposed to happen—that they are a sign of weakness. If someone makes a mistake, the idea is not to help but to demonstrate superiority. These street values can only be changed by teachers who actively teach children that we all learn by making mistakes. Indeed, there can be no learning without mistakes. The surest way to teach children and youth to accept their fallibility is to select and prepare teachers who accept their own.

Emotional and Physical Stamina

Life in the classroom does not occur in weeks, days, or even hours. It consists of intense periods of a few minutes, or even a few seconds, of endless interactions. To say that this is exhausting and draining is to refer to Niagara Falls as damp.

Stamina is a quality that is frequently taken for granted unless it is lacking. In an earlier section, teachers were described as relating closely with children and feeling pain when youngsters in whom they had invested themselves experienced personal tragedies. Injuries, abuse, even death are facts of daily life among children in poverty. Also, after they leave elementary school, teachers frequently deal with students who are pregnant, on drugs, or in gangs, or who have dropped out and disappeared. All of these tragedies are deeply felt by teachers who have established close relationships with children and their families. Star teachers frequently report that they are on a first-name basis or have become friendly with parents and/or other relatives of their students. But they are able to go on, to continue to reach out and support children, regardless of the disappointments that befall their students and former students. Such teachers are resuscitated by the successes and good things that happen to other students.

This stamina undergirds the enthusiasm that is readily observable in stars' daily behavior. Stars—as opposed to those who burn out—are vitally "into" whatever they teach. Their enthusiasm for the subject, the activity, and the children's responses are all intertwined. Stars never go through the motions of teaching, nor are they aloof purveyors. They never simply cover material in a detached manner. They have seemingly endless energy and interest in what they are doing. Children learning for the first time what things sink and what things float easily believe that their star teacher is dropping a pencil into a glass of water for the first time.

Chapter 3

In former times, those who sought to explain this attribute used terms such as "surgent" or "dynamic" personality. This is not necessarily a dimension of personality at all. Many star teachers do not claim to demonstrate the same enthusiasm in other spheres of their lives that they show in their teaching. A basic principle of their teaching is, "You can't teach what you don't care about to people you don't care about." In listening to their explanations of what they enjoy most about teaching, stars frequently refer to the "aha" reaction. They talk about the light in a child's eyes, a smile, even a child's gesture of triumph when a concept is grasped or a skill is mastered and demonstrated. Stars elicit and share this enthusiasm as some of their most cherished moments in teaching. Enthusiasm for their subjects, enthusiasm for their teaching, enthusiasm for the children as they "get" things are reflections of stars' energy. Whether we refer to it as stamina or by some other term, its behavioral meaning is clear because it is readily observable. As with other star functions, it reflects their ideology. Learning is living and growth. When learning is at hand, growth is at hand. As a natural act, it is inevitably accompanied by joy and a sense of well-being that is identified by others as enthusiasm or energy. I refer to it as stamina because it reflects the craft behavior that stars know they must demonstrate as learning models for children. Children's energy levels far exceed those of their adult teachers. This is natural and a fact of life. If, however, children never or seldom see their teachers as enthusiastic, what is modeled?

This is a function that clearly distinguishes stars from quitters and failures. However, I have never been able to use this set of behaviors as part of any teacher selection interview. There are no reasonable questions that can be asked in an interview situation that can accurately assess an individual's physical and emotional energy. Until one is observed in the act of teaching and relating to children for sustained periods, it is not possible to predict this quality. This in no way makes this dimension less critical to the success of teachers of children in poverty. It does mean that we must rely on the seven functions discussed previously as the basis for analyzing who will be successful as future urban teachers.

One of the most common explanations quitters and failures offer for burning out is that they feel unappreciated, and that no matter how hard they try, their efforts seem to be to no avail. Stars can give a longer list of disappointments and tragedies in the lives of their children; however, they can also point to infinitely more instances when youngsters have done things successfully or made themselves successful. It is not simply that one group sees the glass as half empty and the other as half full. Stars see an infinitely bigger glass and are working hard to fill as much of it as they can.

The French use the term *joie de vivre* to denote a hearty enjoyment of life. Stars' classroom behavior demonstrates a joy of teaching. Stated positively, they act as if they can teach anything they care about—and they care about a great deal. Perhaps the most accurate term for describing this quality is neither stamina nor enthusiasm, but irrepressibility. They are not worn down by children.

Organizational Ability

Star teachers have extraordinary managerial skills. They need this high level in order to function because they do not rely primarily on direct instruction. They use the project method or discovery methods that involve children in active ways. Frequently, there are several activities occurring simultaneously in the same classroom or area. Very often children are working in teams or groups. It is not unusual for individual children to pursue a particular activity on their own. What ordinary teachers might regard as too much activity, or even chaos, stars regard as a normal level of activity.

Stars also make certain there are sufficient materials, supplies, and equipment for children to achieve particular learning goals. They do not teach primarily with chalk and blackboards to seated children. What this adds up to is that stars must manage space, time, the grouping of the children, and the use of materials and equipment. They are consciously aware of themselves as managers and organizers of these elements. At the end of a day or week, star teachers are able to reconstruct and summarize which children have spent approximately how much time doing what, with whom, for which purposes, and with what results. They plan for more complicated activities in which different students are doing different things simultaneously. Teaching in this way requires a high degree of "with-itness," or sensing as well as directly seeing what is going on in a classroom. Star teachers demonstrate their organizational abilities on a daily basis. Their skills are frequently noticed, however, on field trips. They are able to manage large numbers of children on a camping expedition, or in an amusement park, or traveling some distance using public trains or airplanes. I have observed such a teacher take 60 middle school youth by plane to Washington, D.C. She took them through baggage, detection, waiting, flying, baggage, transportation, and hotel check-in with less apparent difficulty than some people have taking themselves to the capital.

The skills of organization and management are interrelated with other skills of teaching: knowing which children can be depended on to do what and establishing a high level of trust with children so that they not only take care of themselves but each other. Indeed, several children in every class can be identified who serve as co-teachers. Given the opportunity, such co-teachers may become concerned about the progress of the whole class in completing activities that need to be synchronized. Organizational skills are frequently implied when people assert that good teachers are born, not made. While it is true that these skills are not learned in education courses, they are not inherent in all people. They are developed by particular people in response to various life experiences. These skills are honed by people who reflect upon and benefit from their life experiences.

Star teachers are adept managers of time. They can derive value out of 15 minutes, or even 3 minutes, of students' time. At the same time, they can organize an activity for half a day or a week that will fully involve children. Stars don't plan in terms of what they will do, but in terms of what the children will be doing—alone, in groups, or as a whole. Most teachers, without much reflection, act as if teaching were an opportunity for them to rehash what they already know in the presence of children. Stars think, plan, and interact with children as if the purpose of any activity is for the children to do the speaking, questioning, finding out, testing, writing, measuring, or construction, while the teachers serve as coaches and resources to the children.

Teachers' organization and management reflect their ideology. Stars believe very strongly that children in poverty need other forms of instruction than those based on authoritarianism. The life conditions under which many youngsters live and grow ensure that they naturally come to school believing that "might makes right." They see power in some form—physical strength, the power to enforce, or the power to deny vital necessities—as the primary basis on which children—and adults—must relate to each other. Children in poverty begin school highly suscep-tible to behavior modification and the giving and taking of rewards by bigger, stronger, more powerful adults. This approach fits nicely with direct instruction, since the teacher is once again the authority. Taken together, the package of behavior modification and direct instruction appears to work best for preschoolers and children in primary grades. Children are small. Teachers can readily manage them with external rewards and apparent kindness. There is substantial evidence over several decades that preschool and primary teachers are the most directive, even while they smile a great deal and treat young children nicely—including offering snacks and helping with zippers and laces. Early childhood teachers give many more times the number of directions per hour than upper elementary, middle school, or high school teachers. This style of teaching, which has become widely recognized as the way to teach young children, fits well with children in poverty. It meshes with the backgrounds of many children. If one follows directions and does what one is told, there are pleasant rewards; if not, there are punishments.

Unfortunately, as the children get older, they become larger and stronger. They also find it more and more of a strain to sit for long hours during direct instruction. Also, by fourth grade, the curriculum has taken on more abstractions than were evident in the more concrete primary lessons. The use of spoken and written language becomes more precise in standard forms of English. For example, young children can get by without knowing the exact uses of prepositions. By fourth grade, however, the curriculum demands abstractions and distinctions in how terms such as *from, to, by, of, into,* and countless others are used. The apparently successful preschool and primary experiences offered children in poverty are shown to have failed by the infamous split between the third and fourth grades. It is between these grades that the relative closeness in the achievement scores of advantaged children and children in poverty start to diverge significantly (Walberg 1985). The scores of middle-class groups continue to move upward, and the scores of children in poverty flatten out.

Listening to stars has led me to understand that preschool and primary grade instruction only seem to work because (1) the content is extremely concrete and (2) the methods used match the backgrounds of children in poverty. It is a more gentle authoritarianism, but a directive, controlling system, nonetheless. The bankruptcy of behavior modification and direct instruction are exposed when the children become physically large enough to resist and stop caring about the rewards or their teachers. This breakdown in external control coincides with the fact that the curriculum is becoming more abstract and less based on concrete, low-level, information-type responses.

The organizational skills required to conduct lessons using direct instruction are minimal. True, it is a hard job to implement because the children are resisting, but the specific skills actually required by teachers are minimal. In contrast, star teachers are engaged in extremely complex forms of instruction that require the children to accept a new form of relationship with teachers and others in authority roles. The first months that stars work with children who have previously had only direct instruction are extremely difficult and trying for both teachers and children. The children are very uneasy with any teacher who does not require them to participate to gain extrinsic rewards. The teacher is very uncomfortable with being forced into an authoritarian role by the children. At first, even stars must offer some direct lessons, and gradually build the children up to longer and longer periods of self-determined activity. Frequently, even stars are not able to get a class of children in poverty to begin to take responsibility for their own work until the winter break.

The reason for this review of direct instruction vs. the project method is to underscore the organizational abilities of star teachers. They are not only adept at the project method but at beginning where the children are and gradually working with them to prepare them for other, more powerful forms of learning that really work—far beyond "playing school" with strategies that merely appear to work.

When quitters are asked specifically how they use planning time, they talk about grading papers, preparing worksheets, and organizing their teacher questions. Stars plan by gathering materials, preparing equipment, and/or determining what the students will do, with whom, for how long, and under what conditions.

Effort—Not Ability

As is true of all the other functions, what star teachers do is inextricably interwoven with their ideology. For example, it would be useless to know how they give grades or mark report cards without first knowing how they explain success and how they teach children to explain their own success.

We know that as children move through the grades, they become less willing to try for fear of making mistakes and being embarrassed in front of their peers. They also become less willing to seek help from teachers—particularly if this help is given publicly in view of peers.

Children in kindergarten and the early primary grades typically display unbridled enthusiasm. Most youngsters believe they can do anything requested of them and are willing, even eager, to make the attempt. The process many teachers use to correct children, however, is not value-free; it communicates the notion that mistakes are bad, or shouldn't happen, or cause delays, or make the teacher repeat things he or she shouldn't have to, or are foolish and show that the child isn't thinking. In any one of a dozen ways, teachers can communicate negative feelings in the ways in which they correct mistakes. After enough of these unhappy corrections have been made, the child learns from the teachers and his or her peers that mistakes are bad, and that the surest way to make fewer of them is to try less. As most children become socialized to this "educational" process, their willingness to volunteer is systematically stifled. The enthusiasm of the kindergarten is, by fourth grade, replaced by wariness. It requires several months for an effective teacher of older children and youth to develop sufficient trust so that students will once again risk being wrong in front of peers and the teacher. (Exceptions to this are the children with insatiable needs for attention who will accept the punishment of being considered stupid in return for any attention whatever from the teacher.)

Star teachers are sensitive to this dynamic, which is especially exaggerated among children in poverty and children of color. Teachers of African-American children in poverty consistently report that extreme competitiveness among males begins in about third grade (age 8) and that correcting them publicly risks great peer criticism—even hostility—for the child being corrected.

By the time students reach middle school, they have been socialized by their school experiences to believe certain explanations about why some students are more successful than others. Even though these explanations are ones teachers do not value, they have been systematically taught. These beliefs—particularly widespread among children and youth in poverty—center on the notion that if you're smart, you don't have to study or work hard, you just *know*. And, conversely, too much effort and study indicates stupidity or lack of knowledge. Many teachers who make sincere efforts to help individual children find their first offers of help rejected, and are confused.

Star teachers are sensitive to the ages and school experiences of their students. At the start of each year, they quickly determine the extent to which the children in their class(es) use ability rather than effort to explain success. They also assess the degree to which the class is prone to deprecate one another's efforts. They actively and directly teach the concept that trying and making mistakes are normal and desirable activities in learning. So, too, is the process of correcting, revising, and polishing.

One star teacher I observed told the class directly: "Look, if you're learning to parachute out of airplanes, you've got to get it right the very first time; otherwise, there won't be a second time. But that's not the way we learn in this classroom, or the way we learn most things in life. We learn by trying, correcting, getting it better, trying again. I make dozens of mistakes every day, and I'll show them to you. And if you see one that I miss, I would appreciate your help. Let me know about it." This teacher, from day one, systematically created a classroom atmosphere that emphasized effort and deemphasized children's notions of native ability that somehow should lead them to knowing content without engaging in the hard work of studying, thinking, trying, correcting, and redoing.

Star teachers care about effort to the point that they deal with it in some form in all lessons and activities. They know that success in their own college and graduate studies is a reflection of their persistence and effort. They also believe that, for most people in most walks of life, success is more frequently and more closely associated with effort than chance, connections, or some inherent talent. This ideology is especially clear with secondary teachers who are effective. By high school many students explain success in school and life in terms of ability, luck, family connections, and knowing the right people. They frequently are unaware of, overlook, or deny the effort and persistence that is expended by those they define and admire as successful. By this age there are also sex-linked misconceptions. When males do well, they tend to explain success in terms of their ability. If they do poorly, it's explained in terms of poor effort, or not caring enough to try. For females, it tends to be the reverse. When they do well, it's because they studied, and, if they do poorly, they feel they lack the ability to be successful in that particular subject (Graham 1991).

Star teachers demonstrate their commitment to eliciting, fostering, and rewarding effort in their daily teaching, in their marking and grading, and in the way they discuss their students' work with parents and the students themselves. Their ideology considers no alternative. Consider the lifelong effect of convincing students that success in life is just a question of who you know, or luck. Consider the impact on students' lives if they believe in ability without effort. Studies of middle-school dropouts frequently reveal their naive views of success and how it is attained. When asked about their life goals, they frequently respond with "astronaut" or "brain surgeon."

Star teachers eschew psychometry. They place no credence whatever in any form of standardized or "scientific" assessments of youngsters' potential or ability. They do not believe educational psychologists can predict how much, or what, children can learn. While they recognize that some children are disabled, stars believe that teachers learn more about children's handicapping conditions and what will help them most by actually teaching and "living" with them on a daily basis. You can't start a discussion on I.Q. tests or norm-referenced aptitude tests with star teachers. If these scores exist in their students' records, they may ignore them, or they may set out to demonstrate that the scores are incorrect predictions.

The ideology of star teachers is very much centered in their commitment to individual differences, and to the immeasurable potential of all people if given sufficient encouragement and opportunity. The whole notion of predicting in advance how much or how little people can—or, even worse, "should"—learn is antithetic to their very being. They reject the measurement approach in favor of an almost religious commitment that no one can possibly know in what directions and how far a still-developing immature youth might grow.

Teaching—Not Sorting

I recently took my grandson to be tested for admission to a kindergarten for four-year-olds. His test consisted of recognizing a few shapes and some colors. As a faithful viewer of "Sesame Street," he was able to correctly identify the colors and shapes on the test. Hurrah! Nick was fully admitted to the kindergarten.

As a wife and working mother, my daughter was elated to have Nick out of day care and into a kindergarten of high repute. She warned me, "Dad, you can pick Nick up after school, but don't screw this up! Just keep your mouth shut! Call for him, don't talk to anyone, and bring him straight home!" I promised to pick Nick up faithfully and not cause trouble.

After Nick was attending school for a few weeks, I called for him one day and bumped into his teacher. Introducing myself to the teacher as a retired tie salesman, I asked her why she had admitted my grandson. The teacher replied that he had passed the screening test and was "ready" to learn. I then asked her what would have happened if he had confused blue and green, or if he hadn't known the difference between a square and a circle. Would he have been admitted? "No," replied the teacher, "in that case he would have failed the screening and we would not have admitted him." I then asked the teacher if my grandson was definitely admitted and would not be kicked out on the basis of my silly questions. (My daughter's warnings

Chapter 3

were still ringing in my ears.) After the teacher reassured me that my "very bright" grandson would not be expelled because of any question I might ask, I asked the following question: "Wouldn't it make more sense to admit the children who don't know their shapes and colors, and teach them these things, rather than admit the children who already know all these things?" The teacher looked at me as if I were leftover mashed potatoes. I was obviously a troublesome, ignorant old man. She explained that, when she took her master's degree in early childhood education, she studied both the theory and research of readiness. "Readiness," she announced, "is a concept that helps educators determine who is ready to benefit from school instruction, and who is still too immature."

"Oh," I replied, "I would have thought all four-year-olds are 'immature.' "

Again she looked at me in that sad, tired way people do when they speak to the hopelessly stupid. She went on to explain, at some length, that maturity was determined by the year-by-year progression of normal children through the required stages of child development. I also heard how expert psychometrists had scientifically developed this entrance exam, and that, based on a normal distribution of four-year-old children, my grandson was definitely in the top half and "ready" to benefit from kindergarten for four-year-olds.

I thanked the teacher for her patience and careful explanation but couldn't keep myself from asking just one more question: "Next year my grandson, who is already testing in your top half, will have had the added benefit of being in your class for a whole year. Won't he learn a lot more and be even further ahead of the four-year-olds who failed your admission exam and who have to spend this year at home, or in day care, without the benefit of your kindergarten? Will the four-year-old rejects ever catch up?"

This time the teacher looked at me as if my comment called for a two-fisted reply, but she was counting to 10. I beat a hasty retreat without waiting for her explanation. The message she had delivered was quite clear. I've heard similar gobbledy-gook many times from testmakers, administrators, and teachers. What she was saying quite directly—without using the exact words—ought to be emblazoned over every public kindergarten in the United States: *The children we teach best are those who need us least.*

What has this episode to do with the functions of star teachers in poverty schools? Everything! Failures and quitters don't know the difference between giving directions or assignment-making, and actual teaching. They typically explain how to do something, and then direct the class to complete a series of examples or questions. In other cases they simply hand out a worksheet that includes directions, and questions to be answered. The inevitable result of such all-day assignment-making is also inevitable. Some children know what to do and do it. A second group is uncertain and can do part of the assignment. When the teacher goes over the directions a second or a third time, this second group can be partially urged along. Most of the children in this group will eventually finish. A third group does not comprehend the assignment and, regardless of how frequently the teacher repeats the directions, they are unable to comply. This group also includes children who do not want to do the assignment. In addition to these three groups, the classroom also includes two or three isolates who are not part of any group. These isolates may be children who are consistent disrupters and who do not perceive they are in class to take any direction, or they may be children with various emotional and physical conditions. Some may prefer to sleep or to be left alone. Some may be gifted and find the assignments inane.

The teacher who "teaches" all day by assignment-making and monitoring compliance will inevitably perceive that he or she has three such groups plus several isolates in the classroom. The predictable outcome of this form of "teaching" is that the teacher will come to believe that the children in group three should never have been promoted into his or her classroom, and that the several individual isolates with distinctive needs should also be out of the room and in a class for exceptional children. The reason this failure teacher feels this way is that he or she has defined any child who needs to be taught as a problem who is not "ready" to learn and shouldn't be there, in much the same way as the kindergarten teacher described earlier thought it was sensible to reject children who couldn't count to 10 and admit only those who already could. How much easier and more pleasant it is to simply give directions, and sort and rate the children on how quickly and how well they comply, than to actually have to teach them. Real teaching, in contrast to giving directions or assignment-making, involves engaging the children in wanting to learn, planning interesting things to do, showing how in a variety of different ways, and going over things as many times and in as many creative ways as necessary for learners to achieve. Real teaching, in effect, puts the learner in charge since it is he or she who must be interested, engaged, activated, involved, and set to work in his or her own behalf. How much easier to give directions!

The effect of direction-giving on the teacher is devastating to his or her morale. Such a teacher perceives only those who can proceed independently as having a legitimate right to be in class. Only those who can quickly see what to do, after only one or two repetitions of an explanation or direction, are perceived as ready to learn. In effect, this limits the teacher's perceptions in severe and unrealistic ways: only children who are reading and computing at or above grade level and who are willing to comply with directions "should be" in his or her classroom. When failure and quitter teachers are interviewed, they always cite the large number of children in their classrooms who shouldn't be there. *In urban schools, this frequently includes the whole class, or almost the whole class.* "How am I supposed to teach eighth-grade social studies to fourth-grade readers?" "How am I supposed to teach seventh-grade science to kids who don't know what a fraction is and have no measurement skills at all?"

The answer is *"You* can't." Not because the children can't learn, but because once the teacher defines anyone who needs instruction as a problem who shouldn't be there, the teacher is no longer accountable.

Star teachers, on the other hand, believe that they are there because the children need instruction, and do not expect them to come to school capable of simply following one-time explanations and direction-giving. The bottom line is that star teachers think it is even their responsibility to interest and engage the children in wanting to learn. They not only accept responsibility for teaching but also for making their lessons relevant to students' lives and of interest to them.

As in all the preceding functions, there is a marriage of the function to be performed and the ideology that undergirds it. Before a teacher can perform the function of interesting children in particular activities, the teacher must first believe that motivating and engaging the children is part of his or her job. Before the teacher can perform the function of teaching children at various levels of achievement in the same classroom, the teacher must first believe that the children all have a right to be in that classroom.

Rejecting children who need instruction might be something learned in childhood, or something teachers pick up in their university training programs. If other professionals were similarly oriented, we would have physicians who moan, "Why does everyone who comes to see me have all these problems? Why can't I get people with perfect bodies so that I can just examine them and send them bills?" Or we might have lawyers who ask, "Why are my clients all under indictment or arrest?" Accountants might ask, "Why do all my clients want to pay as little as possible, look for loopholes, and add to my work like this?" The ludicrous nature of the professional in search of the nonproblematic practice, however, is somehow regarded as reasonable by too many teachers.

Star teachers believe they are there to teach, not to give directions; they do not label and sort the children on the basis of their compliance. In urban poverty schools, this is an extremely high-priority function. Without this ideology of acceptance, the teacher will reject his or her students, feel persecuted by their ignorant presence, and burn out.

Convincing Students, "I Need You Here"

For one full year I conducted a research project in an urban middle school. The purpose of the study was to identify the behaviors of great urban teachers. As we proceeded with our work, we were constantly interrupted by the "noise" from the music room across the hall. It took several months for us to realize that the "noise" was a volunteer choir of almost 100 youngsters under the direction of a music teacher named Mrs. Bissell. It took several more months for us to realize that, because this chorus included many youngsters who were causing trouble in the rooms of other teachers, perhaps Mrs. Bissell was an effective teacher. She had an extremely large number of active youngsters coming to her room voluntarily, when they could have remained outside the building. She never had any discipline problems. She never suspended anyone or sent anyone to the office.

After we finally realized that Mrs. Bissell was not "noise," but rather the essence of what we were trying to study, we began questioning her, observing her class, and trying to ferret out the reason for her success. Her choir was recognized citywide, was constantly asked to perform, and was frequently the winner of choral music awards.

In questioning Mrs. Bissell, we began with our preconceptions. First, we discovered she had no teacher education training whatever. She had been playing piano in a cocktail bar when the principal spotted her and helped her secure an emergency license. (Previous music teachers who were certified had all failed or quit, and this enabled the district to hire a noncertified individual.) Second, we learned that Mrs. Bissell knew nothing about the youngsters in the chorus. She never read permanent records or listened to what other teachers said about the youngsters. Indeed, she never spoke to other teachers, since she used her free periods to conduct the volunteer chorus. Third, she never spoke to parents or visited homes. She knew nothing about multicultural issues, and cared even less. The only parents she met were at performances when they came up to thank her for all she had done for their children. Fourth, in response to the question, "Do you derive satisfaction from seeing them progress with this music?" Mrs. Bissell responded, "Heck, no, I grit

Chapter 3

my teeth having to listen to all these mistakes and the way they murder this music!"
Fifth, she did not use relevant material. There was no rap or Hispanic music, not
even any rock. She had them singing old show tunes that she liked, such as "Music
Man," set in turn-of-the-century Iowa and involving four-part barbershop harmony.
As far as we could determine, Mrs. Bissell's entire repertoire of behavior consisted of
standing, banging on the piano, and shouting out which section of the chorus
should come in, sing louder, or sing softer.

After several months of observation, we were ready to admit defeat. We could
find nothing in her teaching behavior that could possibly account for 100 13- and
14-year-olds singing their hearts out for her, without the least bit of boredom or
disruption.

One day by accident I passed her room just as she stopped banging on the
piano. She yelled across to a large young man sitting with his feet on a chair eating a
huge hero sandwich. (Since some of the youngsters came during their lunch hour,
eating was permitted.) The dialogue went as follows:

Mrs. Bissell: Louie, you're not singing. (She stops playing the piano. All eyes turn to
Louie.)
Louie: I'm eatin' my sandwich.
(Pause. Tension builds. Class waits.)
Mrs. Bissell: You could hum. You know I need altos.

At this point Mrs. Bissell returned to banging on the piano, the chorus
returned to their singing, and Louie kept eating his sandwich—and humming.

Mrs. Bissell performed one major function of star teachers, and this one
function was sufficiently powerful not only to compensate for all the things she
didn't do, but to make her an exceptionally effective teacher. She convinced the
youngsters that "I need you. We can't do what we need to do without you. You are
not only important, you are everything."

In the rooms of quitters and failures, the ideology of the teacher is the exact
opposite. It says in effect, "We don't need or want you here. This is my room, not
yours. One more strike and you're out of here!"

Star teachers of all subjects do what Mrs. Bissell does. They consciously create
opportunities to demonstrate to the students that "this is your class, your work, your
effort. Whatever happens here that's good and praiseworthy is something that you
make happen. I need you and we need you. Without you we won't have a project, a

team, or an activity we can fully complete." Creating activities so that the youngster can readily see that the class really is dependent on him or her is what star teachers do. As a result, one of their happy problems is convincing sick youngsters they need to stay home when they are sick. Star teachers have fantastic attendance. Again, the behavior of creating group activities must be undergirded by a teacher whose ideology is that the class belongs to the youngsters.

You and Me against the Material

Those who quit and fail, as well as many other teachers, place the child in a position of battling against the content to be learned. Even worse, these teachers ally themselves with the material, against the child. Learning, or more accurately not learning, becomes a function of the teacher and the material vs. the student. This dynamic is acted out on a daily basis as teachers find they are unable to get something across, or constantly have to correct a child, or must repeat something over and over. They show their frustration at working hard, telling, showing how, repeating, making endless time-consuming corrections. The continual failure of many of the children to grasp what the teacher is "teaching" is fully transmitted to the children. In this form of traditional teaching, the teacher makes his or her frustration, annoyance, and helplessness quite clear. The drama being played out has a simple story line. The teacher is using the content of various subjects to prove to a child that he or she is not capable of learning the particular material—in many cases, that he or she is not capable of learning in school at all. Without really thinking about what this form of instruction is actually transmitting to students, many teachers delude themselves into believing that they are really hard-working and that the lack of student achievement is not really their fault. "What more can I do if the material is too hard for them?"

The daily routine plays out the same plot. A child reading a story demonstrates that he or she can't do it well enough. Explaining the story or writing about it become opportunities for not "getting it." Arithmetic is an opportunity to get perhaps part of what the teacher wants, but there will be more hard things, many of which have little meaning to the child. Most of the day is spent with material that is just beyond the child's grasp, and much of what is learned today is forgotten tomorrow and must be relearned. Tomorrow's teaching will be the same, again revealing great effort—and obvious frustration—as the teacher again explains, covers again, repeats the same content, uses the same examples.

This description is the standard means by which most quitter and failure teachers unconsciously create a class game in which the teacher and the material are pitted against the student. The fact that such large numbers of children will put themselves through this wringer daily for all the years of their childhood and adolescence should be a greater source of wonderment than the much smaller number who become dropouts or troublemakers.

Stars do the reverse. They establish a form of rapport with children that clearly communicates that the teacher and children are on the same side. "It is us, we together, joined in a common effort, against the material, which can sometimes be tricky or difficult or more complicated than it seems. But we can do it together and both derive a sense of joy and well-being: you—the student—because of the thrill that comes from learning and me—the teacher—because I've helped create a situation that will enable you to succeed." Stars are on the learners' side because they do not perceive of themselves as judgmental raters. Their goal of learner independence leads them to use coaching as their basic means of teaching, and coaches do not merely serve as sources of knowledge. They show how, they interest, they involve, and they seek ways to connect subjects with the children's backgrounds and experiences.

Gentle Teaching in a Violent Society

On average a minimum of 157,000 crimes are committed every day in school (Quarles 1989). Approximately 525,000 attacks, shakedowns, and robberies occur in secondary schools in one month (Harper and Epstein 1989). Three million incidents of assault, rape, robbery, and theft occur on school property annually. The New York City Public Schools funds the ninth largest police force in the United States. In 1993 Dade County, Florida, budgeted $14 million for security. In Rochester, New York, teachers bargained for security ahead of salary (Reed and Shaw 1993).

In the urban community, 25 percent of inner-city youth have witnessed a murder; 72 percent know someone who has been shot (Wilson-Brewer et al. 1992). Ten percent of children treated in hospitals have witnessed a stabbing or a shooting before the age of six (Will 1993). In a relatively small city such as Milwaukee, 119 school-age children have been murdered in the last three years. Across the nation, 900 teachers are daily threatened with bodily harm (National Education Association 1993).

The U.S. society is violent, the urban neighborhoods are violent, and the schools are violent. People who want to teach in urban schools must recognize the reality of the situation they will enter. Beginning teachers must recognize that preventing violence is an integral part of their legitimate work; the more effective they are at empowering youngsters, the less violence they will engender; the less effective they are, the more violence they will cause. Beneath the surface and not very far beneath the surface of all urban teaching is the potential for unleashing uncontrollable violence. Only those who really understand the constant threat and horrific consequences of school violence will be sufficiently on-guard to do the countless things that will prevent it. Violence is already smoldering in the children, and only those teachers who see the deep frustrations and anger children carry into the school building with them will be sufficiently sensitive to avoid setting it off.

Five forces influence youngsters growing up in poverty. First, a lack of trust in adults naturally makes young children suspicious of adults' motives and actions. Appearing to be shy or withdrawing from adults becomes a perfectly normal response. (Not expecting or seeking safety from adults or the solution to one's problems from adults might be another reasonable response.) The second force affecting development is the violence typical of urban life today. If those around us are potentially dangerous and life threatening, then it is normal to avoid interacting with them whenever possible. The perception of "no hope" is the third force that characterizes urban life for older children and adults in poverty. It frequently is mistaken as a lack of initiative. If one sees no viable options, it seems useless to expend effort. The fourth force affecting development is the impact of mindless bureaucracies. It becomes natural, normal—even desirable—to give the bureaucracy what it wants rather than trying to respond to it in sensible or honest ways. Only by responding to the bureaucracy on its own terms can any benefits be derived. This attitude teaches children who grow up under such conditions to initiate and reveal

Chapter 3

as little as possible and only what is being asked of them as their normal response. The fifth major influence relates to the culture of authoritarianism. The giving and taking of orders becomes the normal way of life. One's power becomes one's self-definition.

Taking all these factors together, the outstanding attribute one can normally be expected to develop as a result of growing up and living in poverty is frustration. Feelings of deep frustration are a major characteristic of both adults and children who grow up and live the experience of urban poverty. And the result of this abiding frustration is some form of aggression. For many it is expressed as violence toward others. For others it takes the form of passive resistance. And for some it is turned inward, expressed in the multiple ways poor people demonstrate a reckless abandon for their own bodies, including suicide.

The world in which poor children frequently begin school is remarkably positive given their life experiences. Not being certain of or trusting adults, surrounded by family and friends being "done to," living in violence, and having learned how to give and take orders, they still come to school eagerly. It is up to schools and teachers, however, to demonstrate more than a continuation of mindless bureaucracy and overly directive, threatening adults.

The ideology of star teachers regarding violence and what they can do about it is both realistic and hopeful. Their first goal is to not make matters worse. Their second goal is to create a school experience in which students succeed and relate to one another in ways not determined by the threat of force and coercion. Stars work toward this goal by various forms of gentle teaching. As with the other functions performed by star teachers, this is a combination of teacher behaviors undergirded by the teacher's ideology; i.e., knowing why he or she is performing particular acts and believing these teacher behaviors will be effective. The qualities that bring a teacher function to life and make it effective are the unseen teacher beliefs beneath his or her behavior. If, for example, the teacher's real goal is to manipulate and control students, it will be sensed, understood, and communicated to the students. If, on the other hand, it is the teacher's intention to empower the students to control their own behavior, this too will be communicated by the teacher's actions. Teacher acts never impact on students independent of the teacher's real intentions. Students will always know whether the teacher's goal is to control or empower them.

Teachers in schools serving children in poverty have no choice other than gentle teaching. Beyond kindergarten and the first two grades, the teachers can no longer physically control their students with external sanctions or fear. For teachers to pretend they have means to force students to learn or even comply is a dangerous myth that can make poor schools as coercive and violent as the neighborhoods outside the school. Children growing up in neighborhoods where they are socialized to violence, physical abuse, and even death, will not be brought readily into submission by such punishments as a time-out room, suspension, or even expulsion. If the harshest punishments available to teachers and schools can be ignored or even laughed at by the students, why do school officials and teachers continue to pretend they can coerce, force, insist upon, demand, require, or see to it, that the children can be made to comply and learn? The only answers I can come up with are that (1) most educators do not know viable alternatives to coercive teaching; (2) those who prepared them to teach could not or did not teach them alternatives; or (3) most people who choose to become teachers were themselves socialized by power relationships and did not have school experiences derived from their intrinsic needs and interests.

If a teacher, recalling his or her own childhood and schooling, remembers a teacher's disapproval, a failing grade, or a father's spanking as a force that "inspired" learning by fear, it is natural to expect this teacher to be shocked when he or she discovers that today's poor students cannot be made to comply, shape up, and do what they are told by the threat of a teacher's scolding, a failing grade, a spanking, or even a suspension. The fears that such threats can instill today are almost nonexistent to a child in poverty who lives daily with the threats of death, violence, and abuse. Some teachers give up when they see they do not have powerful negative rewards (punishments) that can force children's compliance. Stars realize very quickly they can succeed only by getting off the power theme; that ultimately each child is in control of how much and what he or she learns. "Make" is the critical word here. Some teachers seek ways to "make" children learn. Stars define their jobs as "making" them want to learn. How is this related to violence? In a life engulfed by daily violence, urban schools cannot "make" children or youth comply. They can only select and prepare teachers who will empower students to control their own learning.

There can be no debate about this point. Teachers who start out intending to dominate poor children or youth are doomed to failure. Teachers who seek to empower students may become effective if they believe in and can implement the functions of star teachers. Examples of gentle strategies include the following behaviors:

- Put students ahead of subject matter. Use students' interests. Generate students' interests. Never go through the meaningless motion of "covering" material apart from students' involvement and learning.
- Never use shame or humiliation.
- Never scream or harangue.
- Never get caught in escalating punishments to force compliance.
- Listen, hear, remember, use students' ideas.
- Model cooperation with all other adults in the building.
- Respect students' expressions of ideas.
- Demonstrate empathy for students' expressions of feelings.
- Identify students' pain, sickness, and abuse, then follow-up with people who can help them.
- Redefine the concept of a hero. Show how people who work things out are great.
- Teach students peer mediation.
- Do not expect students to learn from failing; repeated failure leads only to more frustration and giving up.
- Devise activities at which students can succeed; success engenders further effort.
- Be a source of constant encouragement by finding good parts of all students' work.
- Defuse, sidestep, redirect all challenges to your authority. Never confront anyone, particularly in public.
- Use cooperative learning frequently.
- Create an extended family in the classroom.
- Use particular subject matters as the way to have "fights": science "fights" about rival explanations, math "fights" about different solutions, social studies "fights" about what really happened.
- Never ask students for private information publicly.
- Don't try to control by calling on children who are not paying attention and embarrassing them.
- Demonstrate respect for parents in the presence of their children.

The list of do's and don't's can be shortened by simply remembering that everyone needs to be treated with respect and courtesy. Will all these behaviors ensure that violence will be kept out of the school? No. The effect of these and other gentle, respectful behaviors is that schools will cut down on the degree to which they contribute to problems of violence and not exacerbate the violent culture children and youth bring from society into the school.

Star teachers see their jobs as helping to create safe havens where, for a good part of every day, the madness of violence will not intrude and their children will experience freedom from fear. Some other teachers do not have this job concept at all—they simply believe that because violence *should* not occur, it *should* not be in school and, therefore, *should* not be part of the teacher's day-to-day work. Beginning with these opposite views—stars looking at the world as it is and others seeing it in terms of some idealized fantasy—the two groups come to perform entirely different teaching jobs. Stars engage in gentle teaching aimed at making learning intrinsic and students accountable, while the others implement top-down management models the youngsters are bound to resist and conquer by noncompliance.

Only those who have the self-confidence and strength to function in peaceful ways in volatile and potentially violent situations need apply. Many frail, elderly female middle school teachers succeed every day while macho, male, ex-football heroes are driven out. Teacher strength is an inner quality demonstrated by an ability to share authority with children and youth whom most people are unwilling to trust.

When Teachers Face Themselves

To some degree, all of us are socialized to regard our culture group as superior to others. Our group may be based on race, religion, language, gender, class, or all of the above. We are likely to overlay these notions of better or worse groups with factors such as age, appearance, or the lack of apparent handicaps. To grow up in U.S. society (as well as in others) is to be carefully taught prejudices in favor of some kinds of people and against others.

The first step for teachers-to-be is a thorough self-analysis of the content of their prejudices. Which are the "superior" people(s), and what are their attitudes? Which are the "inferior" people(s), and what are their attributes? This analysis will take a long period of soul-searching. For those who go into denial ("I'm not a prejudiced person"), there's always the possibility they may never get beyond this first step. If so, they should not be allowed near children or youth. The second step is to seek answers to the question of source: How did I learn or come to believe these things? Who taught them to me? When? Under what conditions? How much a part of my daily life are these beliefs? This second phase will be illuminating as one considers his or her biography and the significant others who have shaped his or her perceptions. Step three of the self-analysis becomes even more interesting. In what ways do I benefit or suffer from my prejudices? For example, as a white male I may benefit from lower health insurance rates at the expense of others. I may also suffer from a loss of many valuable interactions by cutting myself off from individuals I perceive as unworthy of friendship. This phase is an especially critical step because it reveals the myriad ways in which our daily living is affected by our prejudices. Step four is to consider how our prejudices may be affecting the many issues surrounding what we believe about schools, children, and how they learn best. Do we believe in a hierarchy of native intelligence related to race? Are females capable of learning math and science? Why are almost all superintendents male? Should a deaf person be licensed to teach? Can high school dropouts who are parents really serve as role models? Step five is the phase in which we lay out a plan explicating what we plan to do about our prejudices. How do we propose to check them, unlearn them, counteract them, and get beyond them?

These five steps are, of course, not taught in traditional teacher education programs. Neither are they required by state bureaus of teacher licensure. Indeed, it is now possible to write to any of the 50 state departments of education, stating, "I don't believe black children can ever be taught as much as white children" and still receive a teacher's license, provided one has completed the required coursework and passed a basic skills test.

For beginning teachers to succeed with children in poverty from diverse cultural backgrounds, they must successfully complete the five steps above. Middle-class suburban children also need teachers who have faced themselves and their own biases, but in the multicultural, urban schools, the teacher must pass the most severe test. In urban schools, interacting successfully with children or youth from all groups is not an academic, textbook exercise but a face-to-face interaction. Although the effects of a prejudiced teacher on children everywhere are detrimental and to be avoided, a culturally incompetent teacher who might survive in a small town or suburb will not last a day in an urban situation, except as a failure or burnout.

As if this level of self-understanding were not sufficiently difficult to attain, there are still other self-tests beginners need to administer. These involve the beginning teacher asking what he or she believes about cultural diversity and its role in teaching, learning, and school curriculum.

Only Decent People Can Be Prepared to Teach

The question is what "decent" means. As I interact with star teachers and try to understand their ideology, it is clear to me that they live what they believe. It is not possible to list their beliefs and commitments apart from their behaviors. Just as the functions they perform as teachers cannot be understood apart from their undergirding ideology, the converse is also true.

The problem is that most people who select future teachers, either to train or hire, do not use the definition of "decent" that is represented by star teachers—they simply use their own views of the world. When I reflect on what star teachers have told me, their basic decency is reflected by, but not limited to, the following attributes.

- They tend to be nonjudgmental. As they interact with children and adults in schools, their first thought is not to decide the goodness or badness of things but to understand events and communications.
- They are not moralistic. They don't believe that preaching is teaching.
- They are not easily shocked even by horrific events. They tend to ask themselves, "What can I do about this?" and if they think they can help, they do; otherwise, they get on with their work and their lives.
- They not only listen, they hear. They not only hear, they seek to understand. They regard listening to children, parents, or anyone involved in the school community as a potential source of useful information.
- They recognize they have feelings of hate, prejudice, and bias and strive to overcome them.
- They do not see themselves as saviors who have come to save their schools. They don't really expect their schools to change much.
- They do not see themselves as being alone. They network.
- They see themselves as "winning" even though they know their total influence on their students is much less than that of the total society, neighborhood, and gang.
- They enjoy their interactions with children and youth so much they are

willing to put up with irrational demands of the school system.

- They think their primary impact on their students is that they've made them more humane and less frustrated, or raised their self-esteem.
- They derive all types of satisfactions and meet all kinds of needs by teaching children or youth in poverty. The one exception is power. They meet no power needs whatever by functioning as teachers.

This is not a summary of what makes stars "decent." These are simply a few manifestations of their decency. It seems strange that while so many reasonable people understand that it takes decent people for teacher education to "take," we continue to select and prepare people for this sensitive occupation by examining only their grades and test scores. States have established that a driver's license is a privilege, not a right. Might this concept be extended to the process of licensing teachers?

References and Readings

American Association for the Advancement of Science. 1989. *Project 2061: Science for all Americans.* Washington, D.C.: AAAS.

Barr, A. S. 1929. *Characteristic differences in the teaching performance of good and poor teachers of the social studies.* Bloomington, Ill.: Public School Publishing.

Barr, A. S. 1948. The measurement and prediction of teacher efficiency: A summary of investigations. *Journal of Experimental Education* 16(June): 203–83.

Becker, H. S. 1961. *The boys in white: Student culture in medical school.* Chicago: University of Chicago Press.

Bettelheim, B. 1965. The problem of generations. In *The challenge of youth,* ed. E. H. Erikson, 76–109. Garden City, N.Y.: Anchor Books.

Biological Sciences Curriculum Study. 1991. *Science and technology: Investigating human dimensions.* Colorado Springs, Colo.: BSCS.

Borich, G. D. 1988. *Effective teaching methods.* Columbus, Ohio: Merrill Publishing Co.

Bruner, J. 1985. Models of the learner. *Educational Researcher* 14(6): 5–8.

Center for the Study of Social Policy. 1993. *Kids count data book: State profiles of well-being.* Washington, D.C.: CSSP. ERIC ED 357 110.

Chubb, J. E., and T. M. Moe. 1990. *Politics, markets, and America's schools.* Washington, D.C.: Brookings Institution.

Coalition for the Development of a Performance Evaluation System. 1983. *Domains of the Florida Performance Measurement System.* Tallahassee: Florida State Department of Education, ERIC ED 283 777.

Conant, J. B. 1961. *Slums and suburbs: A commentary on schools in metropolitan areas.* New York: McGraw-Hill.

Costa, A. L. 1984. A reaction to Hunter's knowing, and supervising. In *Using what we know about teaching,* ed. P. L. Hosford, 196–203. Alexandria, Va.: Association for Supervision and Curriculum Development.

Doyle, W. 1985. Classroom organization and management. In *Handbook of research on teaching,* 3d ed., ed. M. C. Wittrock, 392–431. New York: Macmillan.

Flanders, N. 1970. *Analyzing teaching behavior.* Reading, Mass.: Addison-Wesley.

Fuller, F. F. 1969. Concerns of teachers: A developmental conceptualization. *American Educational Research Journal* 6(2): 207–26.

Gatto, J. T. 1990. *New York City Teacher of the Year Speech.* New York.

Graham, S. 1990. On communicating low ability in the classroom: Bad things good teachers sometimes do. In *Attribution theory: Applications to achievement mental health, and interpersonal conflict,* ed. S. Graham and V. S. Folkes, 17–36. Hillsdale, N.J.: Lawrence Erlbaum Associates.

Graham, S. 1991. A review of attribution theory in achievement contexts. *Educational Psychology* 3(1): 5–39.

References and Readings

Greer, C. 1972. *The great school legend: A revisionist interpretation of American public education.* New York: Basic Books.

Grumet, M. 1988. *Bitter milk:Women and teaching.* Amherst: University of Massachusetts Press.

Haberman, M. 1965. The teaching behavior of successful interns. *Journal of Teacher Education* 16(2): 215–20.

Haberman, M. 1986a. Alternative teacher certification programs. *Action in Teacher Education* 8(2): 13–18.

Haberman, M. 1986b. An evaluation of the rationale for required teacher education: Beginning teachers with and without teacher preparation. In *Issues in teacher education.* Vol. 2: *Background papers from the National Commission for Excellence in Teacher Education.* Teacher Education Monograph No. 6, ed. T. J. Lasley. Washington, D.C.: American Association of Colleges for Teacher Education/ERIC.

Haberman, M. 1989a. More minority teachers. *Phi Delta Kappan* 70(10): 771–76.

Haberman, M. 1989b. Thirty-one reasons to stop the school reading machine. *Phi Delta Kappan* 71(4): 284–88.

Haberman, M. 1991. The pedagogy of poverty vs. good teaching. *Phi Delta Kappan* 73(4): 290–94.

Haberman, M. 1992. The ideology of star teachers of children in poverty. *Educational Horizons* 70(3): 125–29.

Haberman, M. 1993. Predicting the success of urban teachers (The Milwaukee trials). *Action in Teacher Education* 15(3): 1–5.

Haberman, M. 1994. Gentle teaching in a violent society. *Educational Horizons* 72(3): 131–35.

Haberman, M. 1995. The meaning of the best and brightest in urban schools. *In These Times* (Jan/Feb): 26–28.

Haberman, M. In press. Selecting and preparing urban teachers. In *Second handbook of research on teacher education,* ed. J. Sikula. New York: Macmillan.

Haberman, M., and S. S. Glassner. 1995. Children's literature: Missing and unreported. *Teaching and learning literature* 4(3): 3–7.

Haberman, M., and J. D. Raths. 1968. High, average, low and what makes teachers think so? *Elementary School Journal* 68(5): 41–46.

Haberman, M., and W. H. Rickards. 1990. Urban teachers who quit: Why they leave and what they do. *Urban Education* 25(3): 297–303.

Harper, S. and J. Epstein, eds. 1989. *Corporal punishment in schools.* Malibu, Calif.: National Society for School Safety Center. ERIC ED 310 535.

Hodgkinson, H. L. 1992. *A demographic look at tomorrow.* Washington, D.C.: Institute for Educational Leadership. ERIC ED 359 087.

Kozol, J. 1991. *Savage inequalities: Children in America's schools.* New York: Crown Publishers.

Maeder, T. 1989. Wounded healers. *The Atlantic* (Jan.): 37–47.

Mecklenburger, J. A. 1990. Educational technology is not enough. *Phi Delta Kappan* 72(2): 104–8.

Merton, R. K. 1949. *On theoretical sociology.* New York: Macmillan Free Press.

Merton, R. K. 1968. *Social structure and social theory,* Enlarged ed. New York: Macmillan Free Press.

Merton, R. K., M. Fiske, and P. L. Kendall. 1956. *The focused interview: A manual of problems and procedures.* Glencoe, Ill.: Free Press.

Merton, R. K., A. P. Gray, B. Hockey, and H. C. Selvin, eds. 1952. *Reader in bureaucracy.* Glencoe, Ill.: Free Press.

National Education Association. 1993. *Now: A Weekly Newsletter* (11 Jan). Washington, D.C.: National Education Association.

Oakes, J. 1992. Can tracking research inform practice? Technical, normative, and political considerations. *Educational Researcher* 21(4): 12–21.

Quarles, C. L. 1989. *School violence: A survival guide for school staff with emphasis on robbery, rape, and hostage taking.* Washington, D.C.: NEA Professional Library.

Raths, J. D. 1971. Teaching without specific objectives. *Educational Leadership* 28(7): 714–20.

Reed, S. and B. Shaw. 1993. Reading, writing and murder. *People* (14 June): 44–47.

Robinson-Awana, P., T. J. Kehle, and W. R. Jenson. 1986. But what about smart girls? Adolescent self-esteem and sex role perceptions as a function of academic achievement. *Journal of Educational Psychology* 78(3): 179–83.

Rosenshine, B., and R. Stevens. 1985. Teacher functions. In *Handbook of research on teaching,* 3d ed., ed. M. C. Wittrock, 376–91. New York: Macmillan.

Ryans, D. G. 1960. *Characteristics of teachers, their description, comparison, and appraisal: A research study.* Washington, D.C.: American Council on Education.

Simon, A., and E. Boyer, eds. 1976. *Mirrors for behavior: An anthology of observation instruments.* Philadelphia: Philadelphia City Schools; Research for Better Schools.

Simon, A., and Boyer, E. eds. 1970. *Mirrors for behavior: An anthology of observation instruments continued, 1970 supplement.* 2 vols. Philadelphia: Philadelpha City Schools; Research for Better Schools.

Sutton, R. E. 1991. Equity and computers in the schools: A decade of research. *Review of Educational Research* 61(4): 475–503.

Thomas, W. I., and D. S. Thomas. 1928. *The child in America: Behavior problems and programs.* New York: A.A. Knopf.

Tyack, D., and E. Hansot. 1982. *Managers of virtue: Public school leadership in America, 1820–1980.* New York: Basic Books.

Walberg, H. J. 1985. Synthesis of research on teaching. In *Handbook of research of teaching,* 3d ed., ed. M. C. Wittrock, 214–29. New York: Macmillan.

Will, G. 1993. Medicine for 742 children. *Newsweek* (22 March): 78.

Wilson-Brewer, R., S. Cohen, L. O'Donnell, and I.F. Goodman 1991. *Violence prevention for young adolescents: A survey of the state of the art.* Washington, D.C.: Carnegie Council on Adolescent Development. ERIC ED 356 442.

Yager, R. E. 1991. The constructivist learning model. *Science Teacher* 58(6): 52–57.

Yeany, R. 1991. A unifying theme is science education? *National Association for Research in Science Teaching News* 33(2): 1–3.

Index